Long Distance Paths

Young walkers on the Pennine
Way (*Crown Copyright*)

In preparing this book the author has drawn upon his experience as a
former member of the staff of the Countryside Commission, but the views
expressed are his own and do not necessarily represent the views or present
policies of the Commission.

T. G. Millar

Long Distance
Paths
of England and Wales

T. G. Millar

David & Charles
Newton Abbot London North Pomfret (Vt) Vancouver

The author wishes to thank Steve Taylor, Roy Brown and Jean Jefcoate for help with the photographs.

ISBN 0 7153 7332 2

Library of Congress Catalog Card Number 76-54084

Set in 10 on 11 pt Bembo and printed in Great Britain at the Alden Press, Oxford for David & Charles (Publishers) Limited, Brunel House, Newton Abbot, Devon

Published in the United States of America by David & Charles Inc, North Pomfret, Vermont 05053, USA

Published in Canada by Douglas David & Charles Limited, 1875 Welch Street, North Vancouver, BC

Contents

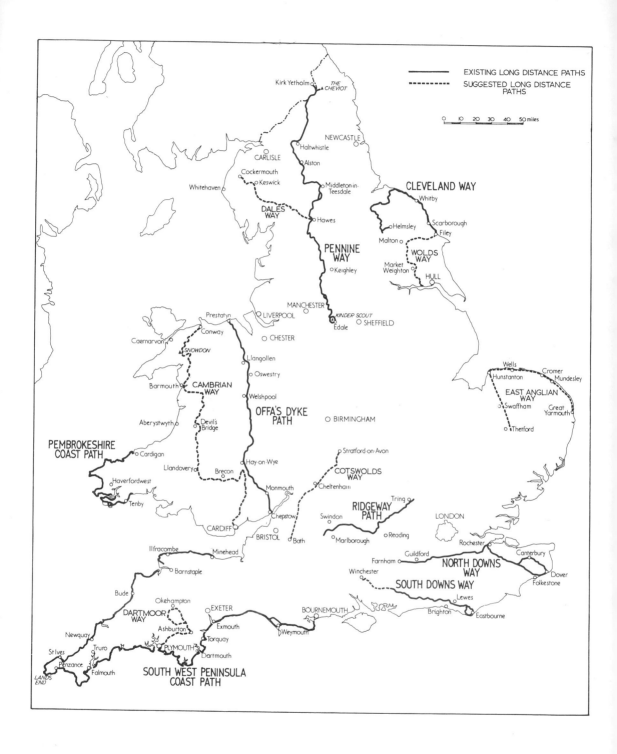

1 · What are Long Distance Paths?

A Growing Interest

Each year more and more people are becoming aware of long distance paths and what they have to offer. Men and women, of all ages, who do not regard themselves as being especially hardy, are attracted to the idea of setting aside as much as a fortnight or as little as a day or two to explore some part of the eight national routes for walkers and riders that are now open to them. The paths take in some of the most beautiful and exciting scenery in England and Wales. Apart from the opportunity for healthy exercise in the open air which they provide, they can be the means to new knowledge and awareness in a number of fields of countryside and general interest.

For some people the attraction is the challenge of covering long distances and the difficulty of the terrain. But not all the paths are difficult and for most people the main attraction is the grandeur or charm of the landscape, with the added feeling of achievement, when the path of one's choice is completed, of having done something worthwhile under one's own steam and at one's own pace. But there is much else of interest on the way. The geology and climate have, through millions of years of change, determined the composition, shape and appearance of the rocks, soils and landforms of the areas through which the routes pass, and these in turn have decided its vegetation and its flora and fauna. People have over the last few thousand years lived and worked in these areas and the considerable changes they have made to the natural landscape through the ages can be observed and interpreted. Each area shows differences in the scale and nature of human intervention, in the styles and materials of its buildings, in its farming and forestry practices and in other uses of the land, down to the appearance of such items of detail as walls, fences and gates, and even in the character of its people.

The Eight Routes

The eight long distance paths are made up of some 2,400km (1,500 miles) of pathways, tracks and green roads, with only occasional short sections of linking lanes and minor roads, running through fields and woods, over moors and heathland, along cliff-tops and across beaches, down valleys and up hill-sides. Each route is continuous and can be followed as of right throughout its length. The routes are in remote and scenically attractive areas, and they avoid towns as far as possible, though villages and hamlets are visited, not only for their own sake but for accommodation. The paths are fairly evenly spread throughout the country, upland and coastal areas being generally preferred to flatter ground. More often than not they take in long stretches of one or more national parks or areas of outstanding natural beauty. Each route has a theme or motif, upland routes generally following a range of hills along an escarpment, where there are the best views. Coastal routes follow the sea edge as closely as possible, often along cliff-tops, but in the case of the Offa's Dyke Path the theme is, exceptionally, a man-made feature, the line of an ancient earthwork. Departures from the theme are nevertheless frequent, either to take in better walking or riding country, to visit interesting sites or good viewpoints, or to bring the route within reach of places of accommodation.

The eight routes are widely spread and offer a good cross-section of the country's scenic interest. The Pennine Way, the first long distance path to be created and the first to be completed, runs along the Pennines for 400km (250 miles) from Edale in Derbyshire to Kirk Yetholm just over the border in Scotland. Three national parks are included in this length and the path, which opens up areas of great scenic grandeur, has acquired a reputation as a challenge for the strongest walkers. The Pembrokeshire Coast Path lies entirely within a national park and follows a coastline of cliffs and small bays which is outstanding for its wealth of sea-bird life and for its wild flowers, and has much of interest in its history, especially its links with early Christianity. The Offa's Dyke Path runs between England and Wales following the course of the earthwork of that name constructed in the Dark Ages, whose true purposes are still not entirely clear.

The Cleveland Way lies almost entirely within the Yorkshire Moors National Park and includes a coast path and an inland hill-top path, both giving exceptionally fine views. It has the distinction of having among its attractions industrial relics which add to its interest more than they detract from the beauty of the scenery. There is also a route along each of the three chalk ridges in the South of England—the South Downs; the North Downs; and the Chilterns and the Berkshire and Marlborough Downs. Each of these three routes is across rolling downland in countryside of gentle charm where green grass, white chalk and blue skies make ever-changing pictures in shades of pastel, and where the countryside is dotted with quiet old villages and extensive parklands.

Finally among the established routes is the South West Peninsula Path which includes the entire coastline of Devon, Cornwall and Dorset and part of Somerset. This composite path was made in sections at different times and includes grand and rugged cliff scenery as well as quiet bays and lonely creeks, fine beaches, wooded estuaries and bold headlands.

Other routes have been suggested which, if created, will provide an additional ridge route along the Yorkshire Wolds similar in many ways to the southern ridge routes; a circular bridleway route in Dartmoor; a route in East Anglia comprising a Roman road and a coast path; and possibly a challenging high-level route throughout the length of Central Wales.

All of the paths may be used by walkers, but the South Downs Way and the section of the Ridgeway Path between Goring and Avebury are also bridleways throughout, as will be the proposed Dartmoor Path. Bridleways may also be used as of right by cyclists, but cyclists must take things as they find them. They must not mind rough going and be prepared to put up with rough surfaces and steep gradients.

What the Paths are Like

The first striking thing about each route is its length, this being one of the greatest attractions, for it makes it possible to spend long periods in places where nature is still, by and large, supreme, and to forget for a time the strains and stresses of modern urban life. The Pennine Way is likely to take a good walker a fortnight or three weeks, but there is no need, it need hardly be said, to travel all the way on this or any other route, or to travel all the way at one time. Few people are, for example, likely to walk the whole 800km (500 miles) of the South West Peninsula Path at one time, and the most common use of this path at least is likely to continue to be by holiday-makers, who will walk relatively short stretches of it.

The scenery, and peace and quiet, are among the most popular reasons for walking a long distance path. About twenty miles is probably as much as most people will care to cover in a day over the terrain encountered. Competitive walking has, however, emerged in some cases and records for completing the route have been established for some paths. The Long Distance Walkers' Association organises walks (not only of the competitive kind) along the paths and acts as a forum for persons interested in this kind of activity, and the Youth Hostels Association and the Ramblers' Association also organise parties along them. In addition there are societies dedicated to the promotion and use of individual routes such as the Offa's Dyke Association and the Sou' West Way Association. Particulars of some organisations likely to be of interest to intending users of the paths are given in the Appendix.

Long distance paths are kept in as natural a state as possible and no attempt is made to make them more than reasonably passable under normal conditions. Thus surfaces have not been 'improved' and although bad patches are repaired where usage is frequent, such as near villages and other settlements, or elsewhere where there is, for example, heavy encroachment by undergrowth, very bad drainage, or where there is a dangerous cliff, the paths are often no more than the bare ground trodden out by the feet of many walkers. The going can be rough, but bad walking conditions are not typical of the routes as a whole, and where the going is really bad it is because it was chosen as part of the character of that route, as on parts of the Pennine Way. At streams the crossing, as likely or not, will be made by passing over a few rough planks or a fallen tree-trunk, or by stepping-stones, though well built foot- and bridle-bridges have also been provided where really needed, including fine bridges over motorways. Many stiles will, naturally, have to be crossed; on bridleways gates are the rule.

Signposts and Waymarks

Signposting is not, as yet at least, over-generous though some areas are better served than others, and reference to a map will in practice be necessary more often than not. But this is in the spirit of the paths, and

Offa's Dyke Path signposted and waymarked at Bodfari (*Crown Copyright*)

most people using them prefer not to be guided at every step but to make use of their own resources and abilities in map-reading and route-finding. Signs and waymarks at every turn would in any case mean putting up so many of them that the natural beauty of the landscape would be spoilt. This is not to say that finding the way has been made difficult, merely that signing has been carried out with discretion. Generally the paths are marked with signposts where they join or leave a road, or at the exit from a town or village, and a special form of sign is commonly used. This is a carved oak fingerpost with the name of the route worked in raised lettering, usually mounted on an ordinary wooden post (see above) or sometimes against a building or on a wall. The signs include an acorn mark, for the acorn has been adopted as the symbol of long distance paths. A simpler form of sign, also of wood, is sometimes used on which the name of the route and the acorn are branded. As an alternative to the traditional fingerpost a low-set milestone type of sign may be seen on open downland where tall signposts would be too conspicuous (see opposite, above). This stands only a few feet above the ground. It is made of a light-coloured reconstituted stone in which the name of the route and the acorn are cut.

In many places the routes run for miles along clearly defined tracks where no signs or waymarks are needed; and along cliff-tops the course of the long distance path is not often in doubt. There are, however, other places where the walker, even with a good map, will be uncertain whether he has reached a point where he should turn off the track he has been following, or which of two, three or more paths he should take where the way divides. To meet this problem and to mark the correct way where the user might be in real difficulty away from roads and villages, or simply to provide an occasional check where reassurance is needed, the acorn mark alone is used (see right, centre), and it may be painted on a wall, a gate, a wooden post, a tree or even a stone. For more permanence it has been made up in the form of small metal plaques in black and white, which are screwed on to any suitable object, such as a stile or gate. This mark does not indicate a direction, which in any case is not always needed, but it will sometimes be accompanied by an arrow in order to do this. This acorn mark has become so closely associated with long distance paths that it has sometimes been used as a name for them, ie 'acorn paths'.

A milestone type of sign

On large expanses of open moorland where there are few landmarks, and in other wild areas, none of these markings are really suitable. In these areas cairns or piles of turf have often been constructed by enthusiastic rambling clubs and are sometimes added to by walkers as they pass. They may reach considerable heights and the stones or turves may be piled round a white stake to make the waymark more conspicuous. The white-painted stake, with the name or initials of the route marked on it, may also be used alone where materials for a cairn are less easily found. Cairns will most frequently be found on the Pennine Way (see right, below). A high white stake may also be found in lowland areas and can, for example, mark the point of exit from a large field which has to be crossed, where the gate or stile which has to be used is not itself visible.

Acorn mark—the long-distance paths symbol

Origins

The idea for long distance paths began, like national parks, in the USA. The Appalachian Trail was suggested by Benton MacKaye, an American forester and planner, in 1921. It now runs for 2,000 miles along the ridges of the Appalachian Mountains through fourteen states, eight national forests and two national parks, and is provided with simple camping sites and shelters.

Tom Stephenson, journalist and secretary of the Ramblers' Association, took up the idea of walkers' trails before the war and proposed a route along the Pennines taking in the highest ground and using the most remote and interesting terrain to be found. The idea met with support when publicised in a newspaper article in 1935, and a Pennine Way Association was founded to further the proposal and to implement the route he had planned. When the Hobhouse Committee on National Parks was set up by the government during the war to examine the need for national parks in this country, it formed a special committee to examine public access in the countryside and public rights of way. This committee recommended in 1946 the establishment of 'long distance routes' (the term 'long distance paths' is now usually preferred) and suggested, apart from the Pennine Way itself, a number of other possible routes, most of which were later adopted. The recommendations of the Hobhouse Committee led to the National Parks and Access to the Countryside Act of 1949.

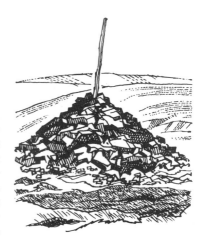

Cairn landmark on the summit of Penyghent, on the Pennine Way

The Countryside Commission

Since the passing of this Act much painstaking effort has been put into the creation of long distance paths. The body responsible for proposing them and for exercising general surveillance over their use and development is the Countryside Commission, which was set up under the Act as the National Parks Commission. Its main duties are the designation of national parks and areas of outstanding natural beauty but also the protection of the countryside in general and the promotion of recreation and open-air activities in the countryside. The 1949 Act made it possible to secure general access for recreation to 'open country' (mainly uncultivated land) and provided the means whereby, for the first time, all public rights of way in England and Wales could be ascertained and recorded. It was in this latter context that the Commission were empowered to devise and set up long distance routes, that is, 'routes along which the public may make extensive journeys on foot or on horseback away from roads mainly used by traffic'.

Some 500km, or more than 300 miles, of new rights of way were created in the process of making the eight routes, to link up existing paths, and in the majority of cases this was done by voluntary agreement with the landowners concerned. The cost of creating the paths, and all expenditure on such things as footbridges, signs, maintenance and repairs, are a national charge and no financial burden need fall on the communities through which the routes pass. The Countryside Commission may make grants for the provision of accommodation along long distance paths and a number of youth hostels have been established with such aid, particularly along the Pennine Way. Help can also be given towards the provision of ferry services, though little, if any, use has been made of this power. Action can be taken to restrict traffic using a long distance path, for example, along green roads included in a route, where a right to take cars may exist. The Commission provides information about long distance paths and a series of guide-books and leaflets are in course of publication. Short films featuring the acorn symbol have been made by the Central Office of Information and feature films about routes have been shown on television, in particular on the Pennine Way and the South Downs Way.

Other Routes

Long distance paths do not exist only in England and Wales or in the USA, where there are also shorter trails than the Appalachian Trail, such as the Finger Lakes Trail of over 600 miles across New York State and the Long Trail of Vermont of 250 miles. The Bruce Trail in Canada covers 450 miles. Long riding and walking trails have also been developed in Australia and there is a highly developed system of *routes de longue randonnée* in France, of which the best-known is the *Circuit de Mont Blanc*, an international high-level route which takes in parts of Italy and Switzerland as well as French Savoy. A trans-European route has even been proposed terminating in Normandy and linked, conceptually, with the North Downs Way.

2 · Using the Long Distance Paths

Preparation

The amount of preparation needed for the practical business of tackling a long distance path depends on both the user and the path. It is as unnecessary to be loaded with elaborate walking gear for a short summer walk along the North or South Downs Way or the Ridgeway Path as it is foolish to tackle the Derbyshire moors in winter without suitable clothing and equipment. The best advice that can be given is that anyone intending to spend a number of days on one of the paths should think carefully beforehand, try to anticipate all the problems likely to arise, and prepare accordingly. It is advisable not to underestimate the hazards of long distance walking in unfamiliar country in bad weather, but if common sense is used no real problem should arise.

The routes are planned to be negotiated by the general public without expert skills or special training, but there are times and places where prudence is necessary. Apart from the extensive high moors on the Pennine Way and limited sections on other routes, such as the Black Mountains on the Offa's Dyke Path, the paths are not likely to be unduly taxing to a reasonably fit person, but hill slopes can be steep, not least on coast routes, and will be tiring in the early stages.

The choice of a long distance path is likely to be influenced first by the difficulty of the route matched against the walker's energies and physical abilities, and secondly by personal interests in its scenic and other attractions. Consideration has then to be given to such matters as how to get there, whether it is to be an endurance walk or a leisurely tour, how much time is available, accommodation, the time of year, whether the trip is to be in a group or alone and at which end of the route the walk will start. Once these matters are settled it will be a question of making a more detailed plan and of getting the necessary information.

The first and essential piece of information about any long distance path is the line of the route on a map. The Pennine Way has long been shown on the Ordnance Survey 1in series, and the other routes are being progressively marked by name on the new 1:50,000 (1¼in) series, new sections of path being included as they become legally established. The inclusion of a particular long distance path should, however, be checked before purchase.

The information contained in the map may be supplemented by written material, which may be either of a practical, route-finding nature or deal with matters of general interest. The Countryside Commission publishes free leaflets about each of the routes, each containing a small-scale map and some general comments on the route, but while these are useful something more detailed is needed. The Ramblers' Association publishes factual route-finding pamphlets on some of the routes and the Countryside Commission is in course of publishing a series of guides, each containing sectional 1in or 2½in maps, the coverage to date comprising the Pennine Way, the Cleveland Way, and the Pembrokeshire Coast Path. Other guides will follow. A list of other publications on individual paths is given in the Bibliography.

On the Ground

The conditions for walking on the three downland routes along the chalk ridges in the southern part of the country are good and the paths are never far from villages, towns and roads so that it is not difficult to get off the path at any time, but villages on the route itself are infrequent and the extra distance involved in seeking places of refreshment and accommodation should not be overlooked. Rain will obviously make the going harder, if more exhilarating, and the wet downland grass or exposed chalk may be slippery on sloping ground. After rain mud can turn a good surface into a quagmire and mud can also be a nuisance round farm gates where cattle have churned up the ground; and there may be marshy ground near river banks. Upturned flints may cause problems for horse riders in chalk country where field paths have been ploughed and not properly reinstated, and for horse riders the crossing of busy roads is a particular hazard. But more serious hazards or strenuous conditions are unlikely to be encountered on these routes.

The Cleveland Way is also unlikely to cause serious problems except on the Cleveland Hills, where there are some sharp ascents and descents and areas of boggy ground. There are rather more problems on the Offa's Dyke Path and on the coast paths and more still on the Pennine Way.

In any upland area, particularly in the north and along the sea coast, there is always the possibility of mist, which can come down very quickly, blotting out all landmarks and making it difficult to proceed at all. It is best to keep an eye on the weather if mist is a likelihood on the hills and to be sure of one's position at all times, particularly late in the evening. If thick mist descends unexpectedly it is better to wait until it clears than to risk continuing along cliff paths or where there may be old mine shafts or potholes or rocky or marshy ground. In rain, cold, wind and mist, good equipment will be appreciated, which will include, apart from strong boots and windproof clothing, such items as a compass, a torch and a supply of food. Naturally no attempt should be made to climb cliffs without absolute certainty of what one is about and in case of dire need. It may be tempting to walk along a beach as a change from cliff walking, but the question to be borne in mind is whether you can get back up at the other end and, if you cannot, whether the tide will let you get back to where you started. Cliff paths also suffer from erosion, particularly in clay,

Typical stile over a rough stone wall

and caution is a necessity in wet weather. High winds and sudden gusts can also be hazardous on exposed headlands, and some forethought is required in unfavourable conditions, especially where there is a steep drop. Route-finding on the Pennines, particularly over some areas of extensive bogland, presents particular problems and these are referred to in the relevant chapter.

Long distance walking is probably best undertaken in spring or autumn when temperatures are lower than in summer and in order to avoid the wet and harsh conditions of winter, though winter walking has its attractions for those who welcome the extra challenge. Summer does however have the advantage of longer hours of daylight, and a cool period in summer, if it can be anticipated, provides ideal walking conditions. In spring the wild flowers are at their most colourful particularly on coast routes, while in autumn the heather on moorland routes will be at its best, and woodlands present their most attractive colouring. Visibility is also likely to be greater in these seasons and this is important for the distant views which the paths are designed to provide. Periods when mist and fog are likely to occur should also be avoided because of the route-finding difficulties and hazards they give rise to. Unpleasant conditions can arise after prolonged periods of rainfall which can make good surfaces difficult to negotiate and bad ones well-nigh impassable. In practice all seasons have advantages and disadvantages and it is a matter of making a personal choice.

It will repay the effort if the map is studied carefully beforehand, either

A useful map board on the Pennine Way at Lothersdale (*Crown Copyright*)

before starting out or as a preparation for each day's walk, or both, in order to familiarise oneself with the terrain before actually arriving on the ground. If one has not done this there may be a temptation at points of doubt on the way to act too quickly and to take a false course, or to miss features which, afterwards, one would wish to have noted. Such features can be highlighted on the map in pencil, because the map will constantly be referred to *en route*; and at home notes of a general nature, eg about buildings, plants, or geological phenomena, can be made on the basis of reading which one has done beforehand. In any case it is best to bear in mind that open hill-tops or coasts, where it is often windy, wet or cold, are not ideal places for consulting documents. A plastic cover for the map is a good idea, as too frequently maps can be soaked into uselessness or torn to shreds in the wind.

Overnight Accommodation

It will always be possible for some users who live near a route to make day visits and to walk the paths in sections, returning home each night, but most people will need overnight accommodation. An ideal method for those fit and able to endure the rigours of camping is to take a lightweight tent, since one is then not obliged to leave the route at all; but there are snags. The weight of the equipment to be carried, the difficulty of finding a supply of drinking water, the chances of finding a farm with suitable land at the right places, and the duty in any event of finding an owner to ask for permission, make casual camping likely to appeal to only a minority of users. The problems can be overcome by ingenuity and planning but for most people the choice will probably fall on the hotels, inns, guest houses, bed and breakfast establishments and farms offering accommodation in the area, or on youth hostels where available.

Strumble Head Youth Hostel

Although out of season it would not be unreasonable to take one's chances of finding accommodation, and with a car the prospects even in season would be fairly good, advance booking will often be prudent, particularly for a party of walkers. After a long and tiring day the assurance of a lodging will make it worthwhile. This underlines the need for planning—the longer the journey, the greater the need. When tackling the severer sections of the Pennine Way in really bad weather it is worth considering, as a precaution, the desirability of a telephone call to the evening's lodgings, giving one's plans and expected time of arrival before starting out. In the smaller places along the long distance paths where the user may choose or be obliged to stay the possibilities of accommodation are likely to change from year to year, particularly in the case of bed and breakfast and farmhouse accommodation, and it is necessary to refer to the specialist publications which are widely published and regularly revised. Among these the *Bed and Breakfast Guide* published by the Ramblers' Association may prove useful. The local authority in any locality, or the park authority in the case of a national park, will normally also be able to give guidance about suitable accommodation in their area.

Transport

The most straightforward, and in many ways the most satisfactory, way of tackling a long distance path is to proceed to the starting point, and at the end of a day's walk to put up for the night at the nearest place of accommodation, and to continue in this fashion until the end. But not everyone will wish to proceed in this way. It is possible to start at either end, or at some intermediate point, but although at least one end of most routes is served by, or is convenient to, public transport, this is not always the case at the intermediate points, and there is the problem of returning home at the end. Some people may wish to skip certain sections which are of less interest to them and to walk the route in leap-frog fashion. It is a useful precaution to write to the bus companies operating in the area for a schedule of services and timetables. If public transport is of no help a taxi may have to be arranged.

For persons travelling alone there are problems in using a car since it is necessary to return to the car at the end of the walk and if there is no bus service the distance may have to be walked twice. But for two or more people it has advantages not least because the minimum of equipment need be carried while actually walking and the driver can meet the walkers at prearranged points for refreshments. Equally important is the greater freedom and wider range in the choice of accommodation that the car gives, and the elimination of extra walking in getting to it. It is important however that the two parties are absolutely clear about the meeting places as there will be no means of communication between them while they are separated. A van can be useful for clubs and large groups, serving as a base and transporting camping equipment to prearranged locations where the site has been prepared by members not participating in that day's exercise.

Other Choices

The direction of travel is entirely a matter of personal choice, but the routes are usually regarded as having starting and finishing points. The Pennine Way is usually referred to as starting at Edale, and the Pennine Way Survey of 1971 showed that most people started from that end. It is worth bearing in mind that in times of strong sunlight it will probably be preferred to have the sun behind one.

Problems of route-finding are bound to occur from time to time in spite of the signposts, marker stones, cairns and waymarks provided. The answer to these problems must be in efficient map-reading and in intelligent observation. It is advisable at all times to know one's exact position on the map and how one got there, and better still to anticipate features in the landscape before one reaches them, so as to have an early warning if things are going wrong. Guessing is not likely to be helpful when in difficulties, and marching off in a direction suggested by inspiration is only likely to make matters worse. It is better to retrace one's steps, hopefully not too far, to pick up the thread where it was lost and to re-assess the problem from there. Normally this will only mean a short loss of time, but if one is hopelessly lost in unfamiliar and difficult country and the weather is bad or it is getting dark it will be wise to decide whether to seek shelter and stay where one is or to take the quickest route to the nearest road. A compass is likely to be useful at such times, and on the moors following a stream may be the quickest route downward.

Obstructed paths, blocked stiles, locked gates, impenetrable undergrowth or dangerous sections of path may be brought to the attention of the county council as local highway authority. Suggestions or comments of a general nature should be sent to the Countryside Commission.

It should be borne in mind when using the long distance paths that the countryside is the working ground of the farmer, and that while one has the right to pass and re-pass along a public path it is important not to do anything which will make the farmer's working life more difficult, and his crops and equipment should not be interfered with. The Country Code should be scrupulously observed:

Guard against fire risks
Fasten all gates
Keep dogs under proper control
Keep to paths across farm land
Avoid damaging fences, hedges and walls
Leave no litter
Safeguard water supplies
Protect wild life, wild plants and trees
Go carefully on country roads
Respect the life of the countryside

3 · The Pennine Way

Opened: 24 April 1965

Length: 250 miles (402km)

National Park Information Centres:

	Ordnance Survey Map Reference:
Peak District Edale—Field Head (Tel Hope Valley 70207/70216)	SK 124 856
Yorkshire Dales Malham (caravan) The Car Park (Airton 363)	SD 901 628
Hawes Station Yard	SD 876 899
Northumberland Once Brewed—Military Road, Bardon Mill, Hexham (Bardon Mill 396)	NY 753 669
Byrness—9 Otterburn Green, Byrness, Otterburn (Otterburn 622)	NT 765 028

A High-level Route

The Pennine Way, 'the longest footpath in Britain', was the first long distance path to be created, and in many ways it still overshadows all the later routes. Its length and difficulty, its ruggedness, its long history, the battles fought with gamekeepers for access to the Derbyshire moors which preceded its official acceptance, and the enthusiasm it arouses among the hundreds of people who now use it, all combine to make it unique among the national long distance paths. It is perhaps its reputation as a challenge to even the hardiest walkers that is its strongest characteristic. The scenery through which it passes, though extremely varied, is by and large impressive rather than pretty.

It is predominantly a moorland route of something more than 400km (250 miles) running from Edale in the Peak District National Park, through the Yorkshire Dales and Northumberland national parks, to the Scottish border, and takes in the highest levels of the Pennine Hills, including some wild and desolate areas where the going can be difficult and tiring. Adequate planning is needed and closer attention to weather and equipment is called for than on other routes. An eye should be kept open at all times for changes in weather conditions, for the open moors can sometimes be dangerous. In fine weather, however, there is no reason why a fit person, given the will, should not complete the route without undue difficulty, though it is a route where on the whole it is advisable to go in a party rather than alone. Some practice in the use of a map and compass is desirable in crossing the wilder areas of moorland and these sections should not be tackled in bad weather by persons who have not done this kind of walking before. By no means all of it is austere and grim, however, and it opens up a great variety of scenery and of places of interest. Walking the route brings a great sense of achievement even to those who decide to leave out the more demanding sections.

The underlying rocks, which make up the landforms met with along the route, were laid down in the Carboniferous period and consist very largely of Millstone Grit and Mountain Limestone, which give rise to

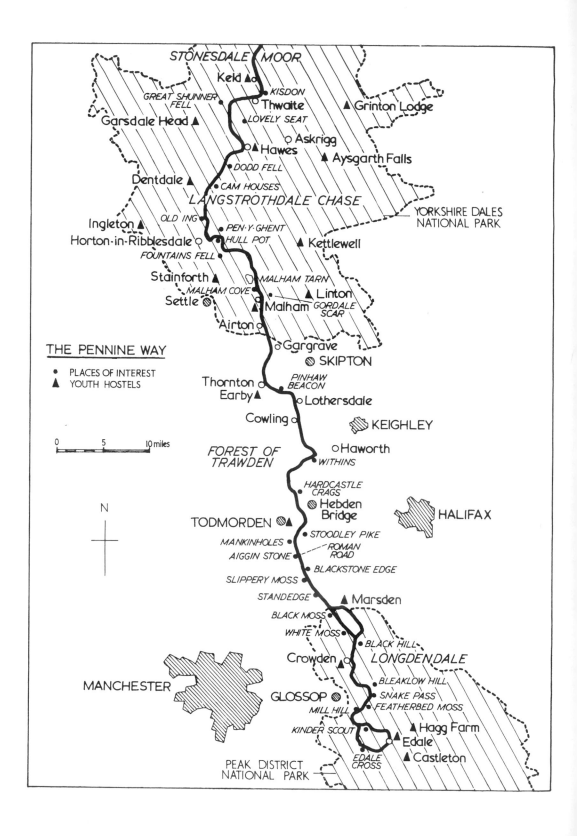

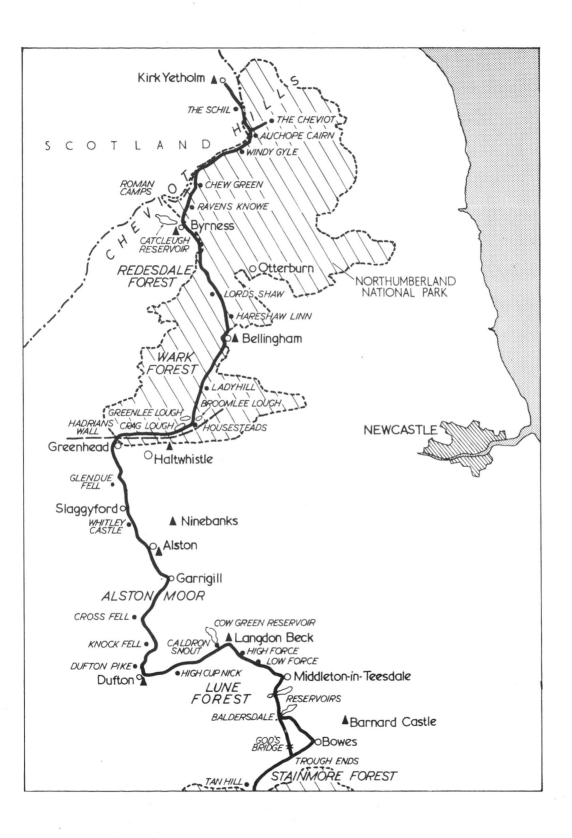

markedly different landscape types. A further mixed series of shales, limestones and sandstones, the Yoredale Beds, appears between these two layers in the Craven area, and is dominant further north; this series imparts its own more variable imprint on the landscape, in some cases, as at Cross Fell, producing a landscape similar to the Millstone Grit landscapes. In addition, igneous rocks make their own contribution to the scenery in Teesdale and near the Roman wall and are the characteristic rocks in the Cheviots.

Millstone Grit

The Millstone Grit overlies the limestone and its presence is evident through the southern part of the route from Edale as far north as Skipton. On the bleak tops of Kinder Scout and Bleaklow near the start of the route dark isolated blocks of coarse rock have been scoured and shaped by wind and weather into fantastic shapes, the bottom parts being sometimes almost eroded away. The fine grains of quartz from the eroded gritstone may be seen on the ground as fine sand, with rounded pebbles of the same material; the sand acts as a further cutting agent when caught up by the wind and hurled against the surfaces of the stones. The exposed grit may also be seen in the 'edges', great outcrops of bare rock, which are a striking landscape feature in the gritstone areas and are a noted training ground for climbers. The rock was used, as the name suggests, for the manufacture of millstones, and a millstone has been adopted as the symbol for the Peak District National Park. Millstones may be seen marking its boundaries where they are crossed by main roads.

The grit, which supported woodland in prehistoric times when the climate was warmer, is now overlain with peat on the high moors, and as the drainage is usually poor the heavy rainfall has cut deep meandering channels called 'groughs', which may be up to 15ft deep on Kinder Scout; or the surface water may break up into numerous channels which isolate rounded tufts of wiry grass as on Bleaklow and Black Hill. In these areas it is necessary to step carefully from one tuft to another to avoid the sodden ground between, and to keep clear of bright green patches of sphagnum so as not to sink into the brown peaty water beneath. After prolonged wet periods it may be necessary to make a detour, still making sure of one's general direction, in order to avoid areas which have been temporarily transformed into marshland. The word 'moss', in place-names such as White Moss, Black Moss or Featherbed Moss, is a warning to look out for such conditions. Typical of the vegetation in these poorly drained areas is cottongrass and *Molinia* grass, the former covering wide expanses in season with a white cottony sheen, giving its name to Featherbed Moss, while the latter tinges with purple the areas where it occurs.

On the better drained, drier, moorland slopes there is likely to be bracken and heather as well as grasses, and bilberry and crowberry will be found. Grouse (see left) nest on the moors and may be raised by the walker as he passes, and curlews will be seen. Sheep-grazing is the main economic use of these hills, apart from the reservoirs sited in many of the valleys to collect the soft, clean water for the nearby industrial towns. The flashing surfaces of these reservoirs often add a touch of interest to what is frequently a sombre scene. Their presence led in the past to the exclusion of the public from great expanses of water-gathering grounds because of fears of pollution, and this contributed to the pressures for more access to

Red grouse

open country and in the end to the demand for national parks. The exclusion of the public from other moors in the interests of grouse-rearing had a similar effect.

Limestone Country

The distinctive and dramatic Mountain Limestone scenery found in the Malham area owes much to the series of earth dislocations known as the Craven Faults and is typical of the landscape of the central parts of the Pennine Way from Skipton to the Stainmore Gap. The grit to the south has slipped and the land to the north has been denuded by erosion of its top gritstone layers leaving the older limestone beds exposed as the dominant land surface. The scenery is lighter and prettier than the harsher landscape of the gritstone moors and of that farther north. The colour of the light green turf is set off by the brilliant white lines of the dry limestone walls and the white rocky scars of the limestone outcrops. The going is also easier. The limestone provides many features of geological and botanical interest and the area is, in effect, an open-air laboratory for geographical and natural history studies relating to this type of region. Where the rocks break the ground surface, as at the top of Malham Cove, limestone pavements occur, and in the cracks between the fissured limestone blocks there is in season a profusion of wild flowers, ferns, and sub-alpine plants eking out a colourful existence sheltered from the wind that sweeps across the top. Characteristically for limestone country streams disappear through massive crevasses to form underground caves or potholes, as at Hull Pot, to provide opportunities for the sport of potholing, but reappear lower down unexpectedly, forced to the surface by impervious rocks beneath. There are major geological showpieces at Malham Cove and Gordale Scar.

Other Landscape Types

North of Stainmore Gap the more varied Carboniferous rocks are broken through by the Whin Sill, a basalt-like igneous formation of dark hard stone, which forms the northwards-facing craggy ridges along which Hadrian's Wall runs. It also appears on the route in the crags at High Cup Nick and gives rise to waterfalls at High Force and further upstream on the River Tees at Cauldron Snout, where the alternating layers of harder and softer rock produce the steps down which the water flows. Teesdale is even more renowned for its alpine and sub-arctic flora than Craven and many rare species flourish, of which the spring gentian is perhaps the best known.

Hadrian's Wall

North of the Roman wall the Pennines merge gradually into the Cheviots, a separate landscape type formed by lava from a pre-Carboniferous volcano, into which there were later igneous intrusions giving rise to a pink-coloured granite. The heights were smoothed and rounded by later glacial action and covered by peat from decaying vegetation to produce the present soft rolling hillsides. This area is crossed by few roads and supports an even sparser population than the hills further south, the people being mainly engaged in farming the Cheviot breed of sheep. The other main human activity in the area is within the Redesdale artillery range, which takes up seventy of the 200 square miles of the Cheviot Hills. The heather-clad peat moors have some Roman remains and are of exceptional wildness and loneliness. There are some areas of bog, with cottongrass and sphagnum, reminiscent of the moors at the start of the route in Derbyshire.

Safety and Accommodation

The Pennine Way has its dangers, and some prior acquaintance with rough fell-walking is desirable if the more challenging moorland areas are to be attempted. The hill tops can be cold and the wind strong, and there can be difficulties in finding one's way over featureless moors even in good weather, and all the more so when the weather is bad. Good boots, windproof clothing and a good map and compass (and the ability to use them) are essential. The several alternative bad-weather routes designed to avoid the more difficult sections should be used if any doubt arises. It is all too easy to lose one's sense of direction when visibility is poor, and it is important always to have established one's position on the map so that in these conditions the right direction can be taken from a compass bearing. Mist comes down very quickly, and can disperse just as quickly; if caught in mist it will be a matter of judgement whether the best course is not to stay where one is until the mist has cleared. The cairns of stones or turf which mark the more difficult moorland sections will be helpful so long as the visibility is good, but care will be needed even with these because cairns and stakes have on occasion been set up for other purposes, eg to mark parish and other boundaries, and some further check may be needed before setting one's direction by them. For obvious reasons it is best not to make a late start in these areas at times when poor weather is to be expected. It is preferable in any case to leave a reasonable margin for the unexpected with the object of arriving well before it gets dark.

Accommodation on, or even close to, the route is not everywhere available and additional mileage should be allowed for to cover the detours that this makes necessary. Apart from hotels, inns and boarding houses in towns and villages, and the occasional isolated bed and breakfast establishment or farmhouse accommodation, a chain of youth hostels serves the route, and is gradually being added to. The most difficult area for accommodation is in the Cheviots north of Byrness where reliance must be placed on isolated shepherds' cottages in the shelter of the valleys.

Some History and Figures

The statutory report on the Pennine Way was submitted for approval by the Minister of Town and Country Planning on 21 June 1951, but it was not until April 1965 that, at a ceremony on Malham Moor attended by some 3,000 people, it could be announced that all the ninety miles of new right of way required for the route had been created and that the Pennine Way was open throughout its length. The reasons for this long delay were not entirely because of objections from landowners, many of whom freely dedicated land for the path. The small and generally remote district councils who were responsible at that time showed little enthusiasm for the work. They were faced with an unfamiliar task, and the local authorities had no strong incentive to pursue a matter which appeared only to impose burdens on the local farming community without any apparent benefits in return. The practice arose for representatives of the then National Parks Commission to visit local authorities and to encourage and assist them in the negotiations, a practice which was extended and developed on later routes.

The Kinder River on Kinder Scout (*Tom Stephenson*)

The atmosphere of conflict with which the Pennine Way began on the grouse moors of Derbyshire continued during its formative period and a number of public inquiries were held over the years. A right of way over Kinder Scout (see above) was opposed not by landowning interests but by ramblers in 1952, who claimed that it would be dangerous for the general public and that if signs or cairns were erected they would destroy the element of challenge which the mountain presented; the result of the inquiry was the introduction of the alternative, safer route by Edale Cross and Jacob's Ladder. Objections to the line of the route across rough moorland between Lord's Shaw and the River Rede in Northumberland were made on the grounds that a ranching system of farming was practised in which bulls and cows ranged freely over a large area and that with a right of way this would not be legally possible; the result of an inquiry held in 1964 was that the path was diverted through part of the Redesdale Forest.

The Route: Kinder Scout and Bleaklow

The start of the Pennine Way is approached in Edale by passing the Nag's Head Inn on the lane which leads to Grindslow House. When the gate to the drive is reached turn right to the log bridge across Grindsbrook where the Pennine Way begins. As we ascend the valley through Grindslow Meadows, by a well-worn path with the boulder-strewn brook on the left, the scenery becomes wilder as the valley narrows. A short scramble at the head of the valley brings us through great rounded rocks of gritstone and over the lip of the Kinder plateau.

The route follows a sandy 'grough' or watercourse cut in the peat running due west. Still keeping in the same direction it passes several conspicuous groups of wind-weathered rocks on the way to the headwaters of Crowden Brook, and then turns north-west over the sodden top of the plateau cut by many groughs with spongy ground between. Care is needed to step on the grassy tufts so as not to sink into the mire. Round about is a brown and blackish wasteland broken with the dull colour of patches of cottongrass and shining pools of water. The streams meet to form the Kinder River, which is followed down to Kinder Downfall. Here one can rest and admire the view, perhaps pass behind the 100ft waterfall if it is in spate and the wind is not too strong, and feed the

Kinder Downfall

sheep. On some days the fall is a mere trickle; on others, when the wind is strong, the stream of water is thrown back over the top in a mass of spray. If the day is bright the view stretches away into the distance, but there is every chance that the Downfall will be wreathed in cloud or even that one can look down on the cloud, as if from a very great height. As an alternative to this difficult section an easier route leads westwards from the Nag's Head by good paths to Upper Booth and Jacob's Ladder to Edale Cross, where the walker turns north and along the edge of the plateau, instead of across it, to join the main route again at Kinder Downfall. If there is any doubt about the weather this route should be used.

From Kinder Downfall the Pennine Way takes a north-west course along the edge of the plateau overlooking the Kinder Reservoir, and passes the head of William Clough to reach Mill Hill, where there is a sharp change of direction to north-east towards Featherbed Moss. In just over two miles by sheep-track along the watershed the Snake road (A57) is reached (deriving its name from the snake in the coat of arms of the Cavendish family), and, still keeping in the same direction, Doctor's Gate is crossed. Doctor's Gate is a paved Roman road. From the Snake road onwards a line of stakes helps in finding the way.

After rounding the headwaters of Crooked Clough at Alport Low the path nears the trackless waste of Bleaklow, which is very hard going and presents difficulties similar to those on Kinder Scout, with tufted grass, swampy ground and confusing water channels. It is even wilder and more severe than Kinder especially in bad weather and after rain, and some skill in the use of a compass is essential. The Wain Stones will be seen just before Bleaklow Head is reached. Just north of Bleaklow Head, Wild Boar Grain should be picked up and followed westwards. The Grain is left at John Track Well, a weed-covered pool, and the edge above Torside Clough followed, past the prehistoric remains of Torside Castle down to Longdendale with its chain of Manchester Corporation reservoirs. Longdendale is an important channel of communication across the Pennines and besides the reservoirs carries a railway, two roads including the main Manchester–Sheffield road (A628) and a 400kV transmission line. The huge towers were permitted to be erected in the Peak District National Park after a public inquiry in 1962, subject to their being carried in the disused Woodhead railway tunnel which lies just to the east of the route. The walker must pass under the overhead section as he crosses the valley.

Black Hill and Blackstone Edge

Across the valley the route loops eastwards before the ascent alongside Crowden Great Brook, a feeder stream of the Torside Reservoir, via the gritstone outcrop of Laddow Rocks, a training ground for climbers, to Black Hill. But before the route turns north for this ascent it passes Crowden Youth Hostel, the first chance of accommodation actually on the line of the path since Edale. The hostel was converted from a row of derelict cottages with the help of the Peak District Planning Board (all the route so far is within the Peak District National Park) and with a grant from the Countryside Commission for National Park purposes and to serve the Pennine Way. Overnight accommodation and use of the cafe is in this case available to members of the public who are not members of the

Youth Hostels Association, and a higher-than-normal standard of accommodation is available.

Black Hill and, north of the A635 road, White Moss and Black Moss are similar to Kinder Scout and Bleaklow, soggy ground of black peat and marsh where the unwary walker can sink deep, particularly late in the year and after wet weather. It is necessary to keep strictly to the watershed across the tussocky humps of wiry grass to avoid the worst areas. To avoid these hazards an alternative route is provided to the east, between Black Hill and just beyond Black Moss, within reach of the A62 and Standedge. To use this alternative route the same direction is followed as in the approach to Black Hill, and less than half a mile below and north-east of the summit the head of Hey Clough is reached and followed to a ditch which leads north-west to the A635; across the road paths are followed most of the way round a series of reservoirs in the Wessenden valley and back to the main route at Black Moss and thence to Standedge.

From the Blue Peter Cafe in Standedge Cutting the Pennine Way follows the escarpment past Millstone Edge and across the moor to the A640, then by a wall beyond the road and thence west and north to the Halifax road (A672) and on to cross the M62 motorway by a bridge which was built specially for the Pennine Way, to reach Blackstone Edge. Here as elsewhere the distances and changes of direction should be carefully studied on the map, paying attention to the contours and the marked streams. These moors are, however, better drained than those that have gone before and heather begins to take the place of cottongrass.

After the tumbled rock of the gritstone outcrop of Blackstone Edge the path follows a Roman road, which ran from Manchester to Ilkley, for a very short distance. Although the deep ruts in the huge stone blocks are said to have been worn by Roman chariot wheels, and Roman coins have been found, some opinion has it that it is in fact a pack-horse road widened during the Industrial Revolution, and that the deep channel in the centre of the causeway was worn out by a braking device on the vehicles used. The origin of the Aiggin Stone nearby is also disputed.

A further causeway leads from the Aiggin Stone to the White House Inn on the A58 Rochdale–Halifax road and thence the route follows the edge of a chain of reservoirs, or the drains connecting them, to Stoodley Pike, a monument erected to commemorate the Battle of Waterloo, destroyed by lightning at the beginning of the Crimean War and subsequently re-built. It has an inner staircase which may be climbed to the viewing platform for the wider view across the surrounding moors. A mile to the south-east below the hill lies Mankinholes Youth Hostel.

In a mile and a half the route drops down to the narrow Calder Valley, in which is pressed a road, a railway, the river and a canal and many industrial works. Hebden Bridge grew up during the Industrial Revolution and there are steep streets with rows of stone cottages built for the weavers who moved down from the hills at Heptonstall to work in the new mills. The path leads under the railway bridge and across a hump-backed ridge to the Colden Valley just over a mile further north, and over the tough grassy mounds of Heptonstall Moor with Hardcastle Crags, a popular, rocky, tree-clad ravine, lying below a mile to the east.

Brontë Country

On the next moor, Wadsworth Moor, the path enters 'Brontë country',

Penyghent in the Yorkshire Dales
National Park. The Pennine Way
climbs to the top of the hill (*Muriel
B Pattinson*)

The way down into Horton-in-
Ribblesdale

and at Withins it passes the ruins of a farm that has been associated with
Wuthering Heights in Emily Brontë's book of the same name. At Ponden
Hall beside the reservoir the path passes the ruins of a building that has
been similarly linked with Thrushcross Grange in the same novel. It was
from these bleak and sinister moors that the sisters' inspiration was drawn.
The vicarage where they lived is in the village of Haworth, three miles
away, and has been turned into a museum which it is worth leaving the
route to visit for its poignant reminders of the family's history. The village
itself with its cobbled streets and grim stone houses looks as if it has been
little changed by the years.

Ickornshaw Moor follows and then down into Cowling and
Lothersdale. Now the route has taken on a more serene, pastoral aspect as
it continues on its way through small fields and hedgerows to Pinhaw
Beacon on Elslack Moor, where there are good views into the pleasant
countryside of Craven and on into the village of Thornton-in-Craven.
The four miles between Thornton and Gargrave on the River Aire are by
well-established footpaths in a countryside of small hills which are the
débris carried along by glaciers and left when they melted; they include a
pleasant, if untypical stretch along the towpath of the Leeds and Liverpool
Canal.

Malham and Airedale

The path is now finally leaving the tough moorland country of bog and
heather associated with the gritstone. Much pleasanter and easier walking
lies ahead. The bright greens of the lush fields of the Craven area will
gradually replace the dark greens and browns of the wild hills to the
south. The heather and coarse grasses of the acid, peaty soil give way to
the short, sweet grasses and abundant flora of the limestone. North of
Gargrave the Pennine Way ascends Eshton Moor and rejoins the River
Aire which it follows first on the west and then on the east bank through
the village of Airton, which has a Quaker meeting house dating from
1700, and through Hanlith to Malham. Kirby Malham also lies just off the
way to the east, a mile south of Malham. No more than a handful of
houses, Kirby Malham is a pleasant village with an interesting church,
which has ancient stocks and a ducking pond. Oliver Cromwell is said to
have been witness at no less than three weddings at the church and his
signature is in the church register. The celebrated Gordale Scar, a mile to
the east of the route, should be visited. This narrow and steep-sided
limestone gorge with many waterfalls towers in a great cleft to 300ft. It
was a cave until, in distant geological time, the roof collapsed.

The route continues from Malham to the head of Airedale at Malham
Cove, a vast amphitheatre created by the Craven Faults and surrounded
by towering rocks over which a waterfall once descended, but this water
now disappears underground a mile to the north of the Cove at Water
Sinks, to re-appear three miles lower down at Aire Head between
Malham and Kirby Malham. The path passes along the limestone
pavement at the top of the Cove (the blocks of rock in such pavements are
called 'clints', and the interstices 'grykes') and continues up the now dry
valley to Malham Tarn, a 150-acre natural lake where a bed of impervious
shale overlies the limestone. It then passes to the back of Malham Tarn
House, where Charles Kingsley conceived the idea for *The Water Babies*
and which is now a field studies centre visited by hundreds of school

children and students of natural history every year, and rises to Fountains Fell on sheep land which once belonged to Fountains Abbey. It is then but a short distance to the steep climb up Penyghent, 2,273ft, a magnificent isolated hill which dominates the scene over the whole area with its distinctive outline topped by a hard cap of residual millstone grit (see page 29, top). Down again past the deep cavity of Hull Pot, turning south at Pot Hole to Horton-in-Ribblesdale, where there is an interesting church and a very large limestone quarry which provides stone for agriculture, for road metal and for the chemical industry. The numerous 'pots' in this area are deep shafts caused by the dissolution of the limestone by rainwater when it has found a weakness. They sometimes widen out beneath the ground to extensive caverns, as at Gaping Ghyll near Ingleborough, a favourite site for 'potholing'.

Leaving Horton at the Crown Inn by a green lane which we later leave to cut across to Old Ing we join another green track, leading to a stone bridge across the deep tree-filled ravine of Cam Beck and to Cam Fell. The walking is easy. Here we join a Roman road, leaving it to pass along the high ridge of Dod Fell, the very watershed of the Pennines, with Snaizeholme Beck far below on our left into Gayle, where an early mill and some old mill-workers' houses are of interest, and on to Hawes in Wensleydale. Sheep and cattle are brought from throughout Yorkshire to Hawes for marketing and the town is a centre for Wensleydale cheese. A fine new youth hostel has been built to serve the Pennine Way. A mile further on across the river and near the route Hardrow Force, a waterfall which plunges over a projecting rock in a clear drop of 100ft, may be

Swaledale, between Thwaite and Keld

visited and a trip made behind the fall itself. Brass band contests used to be held in a bandstand at the bottom of the falls because of the good acoustics.

Tan Hill

From Hardrow an old mine track is followed for two miles before leaving it to ascend by the path to the ridge of Great Shunner Fell, past the remains of coal and lead workings and down to Thwaite village, a cluster of stone houses in Swaledale. The path is along the ridge and cairns mark the way. Many of the fields in this area have a distinctive form of barn, built of stone in two storeys, the upper storey for hay, the lower for stock. The route goes round the eastern side of Kisdon Hill (there is also a path on the western side) to the former lead-mining village of Keld (where there is a youth hostel), passing the 30ft waterfall at Kisdon Force, and then follows a track across Stonesdale Moor to Tan Hill. Tan Hill is a lonely spot with no houses in sight except the inn which, at 1,732ft, is the highest licensed premises in England, originally built for coalminers but now mainly patronised by passing motorists and walkers. There are records of the working of coal in this area as early as the fourteenth century. The coal was used for lead-smelting, lime-burning and for domestic use, and it was carried by horse and cart over long distances before the coming of the railways.

From Tan Hill, Frumming and Sleightholme Becks guide the walker across Sleightholme Moor to the Stainmore Gap, which now carries the A66 road across the Pennines. But before the road is reached the Pennine Way divides into two at Trough Heads. The main route, after crossing the disused railway line and the River Greta at God's Bridge (a natural slab of limestone under which the river disappears), and then crossing the road, traverses several miles of difficult and boggy country with many small streams into Baldersdale and thence to Middleton in Teesdale. The disused railway line south of the A66 was once the highest stretch of line in England. The easterly route continues down Sleightholme Beck to Bowes for accommodation. At Bowes there is an interesting museum housed in a large castle. The museum, looking like a French chateau and standing in parkland, has important exhibits of paintings, tapestries and furniture. On the main road into Bowes is the alleged model for Dickens' Dotheboys Hall, now a café.

Middleton in Teesdale

At Middleton in Teesdale, a former lead-mining centre, a long stretch by the River Tees begins where route-finding alongside the rock-strewn riverbed causes few problems and where the scenery is outstanding. The tempestuous rush of the swirling waters when the river is in spate is a remarkable sight. In this area the harder blue-grey rock of the Whin Sill has intruded and given rise to spectacular waterfalls first at Low Force some three miles out of Middleton and even more dramatically at High Force, the highest waterfall in England in a single fall, just over a mile further upstream. Here the waters are divided into twin falls by a central island bluff. The rock can also be seen as one passes Cronkley Scar several miles further up, and once again at Cauldron Snout, where the Tees falls 200ft down a long staircase of ledges in the rock. Much of this area is a national nature reserve and is rich in flora, with rare species of violets, primroses, pansies and saxifrages, and the rare blue gentian (see drawing).

Gentian

North of Cauldron Snout the Cow Green Reservoir was constructed, in spite of strong opposition from conservation interests in the late 1960s, to supply water for the industrial needs of Teesside, inundating an area which had a unique significance for the study of successions of vegetation.

Having crossed the footbridge at Cauldron Snout below the dam, Maize Beck is reached and followed until the beck is crossed by a further footbridge on the way to High Cup Nick. Here a magnificent horse-shoe valley, of glacial origin, stretches out before you with a nearly sheer drop of 1,000ft. The views extend as far as the Lake District hills as one descends along the northern rim of the great chasm, which is edged with huge rocks of the Whin Sill, to the bright, colour-washed village of Dufton, with its wide, tree-lined main street and broad village green and the conical hill of Dufton Pike towering above it. The area is also remarkable for a localised wind, the Helm, which sweeps down fiercely in winter from Cross Fell to displace the warmer air on the lower ground beneath the hills. As the warmer air rises it forms a cloud above the edge of the hills.

Cross Fell

In the nine miles between Dufton and Cross Fell, which involves a steep climb up the face of the hills, one sees evidence of the great geological fault in which the land to the west slipped to form the high scarp of the Pennines, the land then sloping gradually away to the east. The dark rocks of the Pennines contrast with the red sandstones of the Eden Valley to the west and the slates of Knock Pike and other outlying hills at their feet. This section includes the smooth tops of Knock Fell, and then Great and Little Dun Fells, the former with a radio mast as a landmark. Cross Fell, at nearly 3,000ft the highest hill in the Pennines, is a flat-topped and wind-swept wilderness of bog moss and cottongrass where attention needs to be paid to navigation. Originally called Fiends Fell, the story has it that St Augustine caused a cross to be placed on the hill-top to banish the evil spirits that dwelt there. A watch should be kept for the cairns which mark the way and in particular the large one on the summit; the way down lies north-north-west to avoid the scree and leads to an old mine track. The views from Cross Fell are very extensive and the peaks of the Lake District, Cheviot and Penyghent may be picked out.

The Pennine Way reaches the River Tyne from Cross Fell across Alston Moor where there are many old lead workings and pieces of Blue John, the form of fluorspar more closely associated with Castleton in the Peak District, may be found. From Garrigill the path follows the river northwards through a land of green pastures which contrast with the brown starkness of the moors, to Alston, the highest market town in England. Alston has steep streets and some old buildings dating from the prosperous days when zinc, copper, lead and silver sustained the economy of the area. North of Alston the line still runs parallel to the river, but now at some distance from its banks to follow parts of the Maiden Way, along the fell-sides, past the Roman station of Whitley Castle, for a distance of some nine miles leading eventually to Greenhead and Hadrian's Wall, at the Nine Nicks of Thirlwall. The track of the Maiden Way, a Roman road, may be discerned ahead by the different colouring of the vegetation. On the way the path goes through the villages of Kirkhaugh and Slaggyford and crosses a number of burns, which flow into the Tyne. The placenames from here northwards have a distinctive Scottish ring.

The Roman Wall

Hadrian's Wall (see below) was built in AD125, after the Romans had withdrawn from earlier conquests in Scotland, and joins the Solway Firth to Wallsend, a distance of over seventy Roman miles. It was considerably higher than its present maximum of 9ft, probably 20ft high and 10ft broad, the interior being filled with rubble. There were seventeen forts along its length and at every Roman mile between them a smaller fort or 'mile-castle', with signalling points between them. North of the wall was a wide and deep ditch for greater defence and south of it the *vallum* which is thought to have been a boundary line to the military complex. Between the *vallum* and the wall was a military way, connecting the various strong-points on the wall.

The route follows the wall for nine miles and provides fine views northwards over rolling moors and dark green forests. Even in its diminished state the wall is highly evocative of a distant and glorious period in history, and is itself a thing of beauty, as it lopes majestically from crag to crag into the distance. It reaches its highest point at Winshields Crag at 1,230ft. Half a mile to the south-east is the Once Brewed Youth Hostel which includes an information centre for the Northumberland National Park.

Just before the Pennine Way leaves the wall to turn northwards through

The Pennine Way follows the line of Hadrian's Wall (*Ramblers Association*)

the Forestry Commission plantations of Kielder Forest, first planted in 1926, there are a number of attractive lakes, Crag Lough, Greenlee Lough and Brownlee Lough, formed when the ice sheets scooped out the softer material from the Whin Sill. Near this point is also Housesteads Fort, with much visual evidence of military life in Roman times and a small museum. There are good views along the wall from the fort, which housed 1,000 troops and included a hospital, granaries and baths as well as barracks; outside the fort was a civil settlement with an inn and shops. Passing between Greenlee and Brownlee Loughs in their serene and beautiful setting below the crags and the wall, the way continues by forest rides and across bare heather moors to Bellingham, crossing numerous streams on the way. Legend has it that Conigns Cross, passed three miles from the wall, was erected to the memory of a chieftain killed by King Arthur's sons. King Arthur is himself said to be sleeping in a cave among the crags.

Redesdale

Bellingham is pleasantly situated on the North Tyne river. St Cuthbert's Church is celebrated for its heavy stone roof and St Cuthbert's Well is reputed to have healing powers. The town lay in the path of Scottish raiders in the times of the border conflicts and the countryside suffered from local marauding moss-troopers. It is the last sizeable place on the route, and beyond it the opportunities for accommodation are limited though there are some hotels, guest houses and a youth hostel at or near Byrness, some fifteen miles further on. From the town the path ascends to the heather of Albany Rigg and on to Lough Shaw on a line parallel to Hareshaw Linn where in a narrow glen there is a waterfall with a 100ft drop which is worth a slight diversion. The path continues across rough moorland of tufted grass and heather over Deer Play and Lord's Shaw to Padon Hill, where there is a monument to a Scottish covenanter, and continues along a fence to the east of the Forestry Commission road before meeting and entering Redesdale Forest, where it follows forest rides down to the River Rede at Blakehopeburnhaugh. Across to the east from Padon Hill but some three miles from the route is the village of Otterburn and the site, in 1388, of the battle famed in border ballads where the chief protagonists were Earl Douglas and Sir Henry Percy. The banks of the Rede lead to Byrness.

The Cheviots

Ahead lies the last formidable section of the route across the trackless moors of the Cheviot Hills where, for some twenty-seven miles, the only chance of finding accommodation is to descend into the valleys of the Upper Coquet, where there are a few farms which take in visitors. The scenery is as wild and lonely as any on the route and as in other moorland areas tufted grass hummocks and tangled heather and boggy patches make the going hard and tiring and constant attention is needed to where one puts one's feet. A watch also needs to be kept on the weather. Habitations of any kind are few and the way is rough and also wet in places. The route ascends from Byrness by a forest ride and on to the grassland near Windy Crag and thence to Ravens Knowe and the border fence and the square outline of Chew Green Roman camp. This was an extensive fortification on the Roman route of Dere Street from York into Scotland and the path follows the Roman road for a short distance. The route, which is marked

Scotland–England border sign

34

by cairns in this area, borders the Redesdale artillery range, but is open at all times. The border fence is then followed along the crest of the hills with views over the Scottish hills and down steep-sided dry glacial valleys on either side. Hill-top succeeds hill-top, one after the other—Lamb Hill, Beefstand Hill, Mozie Law and Windy Gyle. A spur will take the walker who is so inclined to the great flat top of the volcanic peat bog of The Cheviot at 2,676ft. The route finally descends and ends at Kirk Yetholm in Scotland.

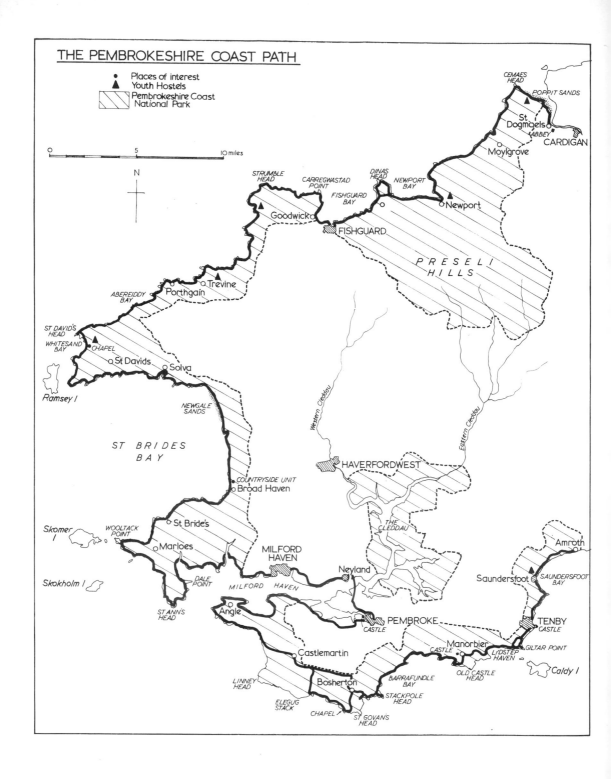

THE PEMBROKESHIRE COAST PATH

- • Places of interest
- ▲ Youth Hostels
- Pembrokeshire Coast National Park

0 ———— 5 ———— 10 miles

N

CEMAES HEAD
POPPIT SANDS
St Dogmaels
ABBEY
CARDIGAN
Moylgrove

STRUMBLE HEAD
CARREGWASTAD POINT
DINAS HEAD
NEWPORT BAY
FISHGUARD BAY
Goodwick
FISHGUARD
Newport

PRESELI HILLS

ABEREIDDY BAY
Porthgain
Trevine

ST DAVID'S HEAD
WHITESAND BAY
CHAPEL
St Davids
Solva

Ramsey I

NEWGALE SANDS

Western Cleddau
Eastern Cleddau

ST BRIDES BAY

HAVERFORDWEST

COUNTRYSIDE UNIT
Broad Haven

Skomer I
WOOLTACK POINT
St Bride's
Marloes

THE CLEDDAU

Amroth

MILFORD HAVEN
Neyland
Saundersfoot
SAUNDERSFOOT BAY

Skokholm I

DALE POINT
MILFORD HAVEN

ST ANN'S HEAD
Angle

PEMBROKE
CASTLE
Manorbier
CASTLE
TENBY
CASTLE
GILTAR POINT
LYDSTEP HAVEN
Caldy I

Castlemartin
OLD CASTLE HEAD

LINNEY HEAD
BARRAFUNDLE BAY
Bosherton
STACKPOLE HEAD

ELEGUG STACK
CHAPEL
ST GOVANS HEAD

4 · The Pembrokeshire Coast Path

Opened: 16 May 1970

Length: 167 miles (269km)

National Park Information Centres:

	Ordnance Survey Map Reference:
Tenby The Norton (Tel 3510)	SN 133 008
Pembroke Castle Terrace (Tel 2148)	SM 983 016
Broadhaven Pembrokeshire Countryside Unit, The Car Park (Tel 412)	SM 864 140
St David's The City Hall (Tel 392)	SM 754 253
Fishguard Town Hall, Fishguard (Tel 3484)	SM 958 370

Cliffs, Birds and Wild Flowers

This path runs along the entire coastline of the former county of Pembroke (now part of Dyfed) for 267km (167 miles), leaving out only the offshore islands and the eastern reaches of Milford Haven, where this deep inlet branches out into the two long and meandering Cleddau rivers. It is thus within the Pembrokeshire Coast National Park, to whose scenic attractions it is a main means of access. It runs from Amroth at the former Carmarthen boundary in the south, round seemingly innumerable bays and headlands and penetrating many creeks and inlets as it follows the twists and turns of the coast, to St Dogmaels at the former Cardigan boundary in the north. The whole coastline has also been defined as Heritage Coast.

The path is almost entirely on cliff-tops and the coastal scenery is among the best in Wales. The cliffs sometimes fall sheer and spectacularly to the sea, the layered and folded rocks in the south being strikingly beautiful as one coloured band succeeds, and sometimes overlies, another, while the darker, angular rocks in the north are no less remarkable in their subtler hues of grey, brown and dark purple. There are sandy bays and long beaches, quiet backwaters, expanses of jagged rocks and always wide sea views. One of the greatest attractions of the path is the richness of its flora. The mild climate stimulates the early growth of wild flowers which appear in profusion from the early months of the year and make the path in spring the most colourful of the long distance paths. Even more remarkable is the number and variety of sea-bird species. The birds nest on the cliffs and in particular cluster on the faces of the stacks and islands which lie offshore and make this coastline one of the most rewarding for the observation of sea-birds. Of hardly less interest are the associations of the area with the early Celtic Church.

Geology

The coast that the path follows is in general flattish, broken in places by valleys where rivers have incised the edges of the plateau which is the dominant landscape feature of the peninsula as a whole. In landforms, as in

Puffin

other respects, there is a marked difference between the north and the south coasts. Geologically the northern coastline is made up of igneous and other rocks of very great age, including those of the earliest, pre-Cambrian, era, as well as of later Ordovician and Silurian times, which are resistant to erosion, while those in the south are sedimentary rocks of the more recent Carboniferous series. When in the course of geological time the area became submerged beneath the sea the softer, sedimentary rocks of the south, having in the meantime been subjected to folding, succumbed to the planing effects of wave action, which the harder northern rocks were able to resist. When the sea retreated the land in the south had been smoothed down to a level surface, and subsequent coast erosion has revealed the edges of the plateau as bands of limestone, sandstone, coal measures and grit, horizontal in places but often folded in synclines and anticlines or even up-ended vertically. These bands are laid down in such a way that on north–south coasts there is a recurring succession from one to the other as one walks along the cliffs and this produces a great variety of landscape and vegetation types. Continuing sea action has isolated numerous free-standing pillars, or 'stacks'. In the north, however, the Preseli Hills, visible from practically every part of Pembroke, stand out above the plateau, and here small streams fall precipitously over a wilder and much less indented coastline. The other most striking feature of the coast is the great deep-water estuary of Milford Haven, a former river valley drowned in one of the several falls of the land surface below sea-level.

The few trees along the coast lean heavily to leeward or eke out a meagre existence in places facing away from the strong winds that blow in from the Atlantic. Brambles, bracken, heather and gorse grow along the cliff-tops, and thrift, bluebells, primroses, campions, sage, sorrel and sea pinks flourish in their separate niches.

Skomer Island is a national nature reserve, Ramsey Island and Grassholm are reserves of the Royal Society for the Protection of Birds and Skokholm is also an important ornithological station, noted for its storm petrels and shearwaters. The islands may be visited and guillemots, gannets, choughs, fulmars, puffins, oyster-catchers and kittiwakes may be seen. But the walker will find plenty to interest him on the cliffs of the mainland.

Remains of the megalithic period—dolmens, standing stones and stone circles may be seen in the St David's peninsula, though not on the path itself. But evidence of early human settlements of the Iron Age—by peoples who came from the Continent by sea about 3000BC—is widespread along the path, many headlands being occupied by circular embankments or by single or double defensive earthworks across the headland's narrow neck.

Christians and Normans

In the sixth and seventh centuries AD Pembroke was a centre of the Celtic Church. Sea-going curraghs, rowed or at best with a small sail, came and went between the parts of the scattered Celtic world in Ireland, Cornwall, Brittany and Wales. The journeys were long and perilous but the faith of the wayfarers was strong and shrines and chapels were established in thanksgiving at the points of landing. The names of the saints and missionaries are commemorated profusely along the coast particularly in the north, and the remains of their chapels may be seen, eg St Justinians opposite Ramsey Island, St Brynoch at Dinas Island or St Degans west of Fishguard. Others on Ramsey Island and at Whitesand Bay have disappeared. From these scattered landing places, dictated more by the winds than the wishes of the wayfarers, missionaries and pilgrims converged inland to the site of St David's ascetic community. Here the cathedral was built in a depression where it would not be seen by the marauding Norsemen who ruled the Irish Sea from Dublin, Waterford, Wexford and the Isle of Man in the following centuries. Norse placenames survive, particularly the names of the islands, Skomer, Skokholm, Ramsey, Grassholm, Caldy and the Angle Peninsula; and in Milford Haven (Milford, Haverfordwest, Herbrandston); sailing up the deep and narrow Haven the Norsemen must have been reminded of their native or ancestral fjords. The cathedral was in fact destroyed in AD999.

The Normans quickly penetrated along the lower south coast of Pembroke as their first foothold in Wales (and as their stepping stone to Ireland) and soon occupied the whole southern part of the peninsula. They built a line of castles (the *landsker*) running eastwards from the north of St Brides Bay to Amroth, which marks the dividing line between the Welsh-speaking north and the English-speaking south. Settlers from Flanders and Ireland were introduced to work the land. The division between north and south still persists. On the north coast the stone-built farms are scattered, the soil is poor and the settlements small, while the richer south is gayer and more colourful, with towns and villages reminiscent of those in England, giving rise to Daniel Defoe's description of the area as 'Little England beyond Wales'.

Industrial Development

In the 1960s the exceptionally deep waters of Milford Haven proved attractive to the international oil companies who were seeking berthing places for the large tankers which were then beginning to be built. Oil refineries and jetties have now been established by the major companies on both shores, and the Haven is constantly being deepened to take ever larger tonnages. Welcomed by some for the employment they provide, these installations and the shipping they bring have altered the character of the Haven. In spite of the efforts of landscape consultants the refineries cannot be effectively concealed or screened.

Few navigational difficulties should be met with in walking the route, but at Castlemartin and Manorbier extensive services training areas deny use of the coast to the public either at all times or when firing is taking place. The county council has gone to some trouble to define the path, which is also signed and waymarked. The council also publishes sectional leaflets on the path, each containing a map and notes on matters of interest.

The Route: Amroth to Tenby

The Pembroke Coast Path starts on the road at the village of Amroth above a long stretch of sands, where the main practices were carried out for the landings in Europe in World War II. The actual starting point is at the stream just east of Amroth Castle. The castle, now a farm, is modern but a mound indicates that this was the site of a Norman, or earlier, settlement. The sea has advanced landward over the years, and occasionally at low tides one may see the black stumps and roots of trees, the remains of an ancient forest noted by Giraldus Cambrensis as early as 1183. Evidence of prehistoric settlements has been discovered. We are here in the area of the coal measures which overlie the millstone grit, which in turn overlies limestone, in a succession familiar from Carboniferous deposits elsewhere, but on this coast revealed in rapid sequence because of the severe folding of the rocks before erosion took place.

The road is left by a bridlepath over shelving cliffs to join the Stepaside road near Wiseman's Bridge, followed by more road and then by the well-kept paths below the modern Hean Castle and on into Saundersfoot on the track of an old colliery tramway. The mines run out to sea but are no longer worked; coal shipments have ceased and little evidence remains that coal was ever worked in the area. The path may be said to begin effectively at Saundersfoot. It climbs up from the harbour, built in 1829 for the coal trade and in particular for exports from the anthracite mines inland at Kilgetty, through the woods to Monkstone Point. It is also possible to start at the signed path a short distance out of the town along the road to Tenby; the paths come together very quickly. The woods here survive because of the shelter provided by the eastward-facing coast, away from the stormy north and west winds. The open cliff-top soon gives seaward views and, once Monkstone Point is passed, views down to the harbour in Tenby. After Waterwynch Cwm we continue along Waterwynch Lane, cut off from the sea, down into the town. Colourful and historic, Tenby has an indefinable lightness and charm. Its massive thirteenth-century curtain walls complete with towers were built by the Earls of Pembroke as Lords Marcher. Settled by Flemings introduced by the Normans, and earning its living in the past from fishing, weaving and the wool trade, it is now crowded with visitors in summer, but its graceful architecture and delicately colour-washed buildings, very un-Welsh in appearance, make it very attractive at all times. Caldy Island may be visited by boat from the harbour. Its modern Cistercian monastery (1907–1911) on the site of a Benedictine foundation, its sixth-century Celtic Church and its natural beauties are well worth seeing.

The path leaves Tenby by way of South Sands, along the beach or at the edge of the dunes (The Burrows) fronting the golf course, to Giltar Point, but when Penally rifle range is in operation it will be necessary to take the path along the railway line to Penally village. When the railway was built it formed a barrier against which the dunes, now used as a golf course, have accumulated and created Tenby Marsh behind it by impeding the drainage. The marsh produces a rich profusion of wild flowers.

Lydstep Haven to St Govan's

From Giltar Point the path follows closely the tops of the limestone cliffs, where there are a number of caves (Hoyle's Mouth is of archaeological as well as geological interest) and blowholes where the sea comes roaring up in clouds of spray in times of high wind and heavy seas. Lydstep Haven is the first of many sandy bays along this coast. Choughs (see left) nest in the caves and seals seek out their depths to bear their young. At this point it may be necessary to skirt the Manorbier camp and artillery range by taking the road to Lydstep village, thus missing out Old Castle Head and the coves of Skrinkle Haven. (Local information should be sought—when there is no firing the path to Skrinkle Haven is available.) The ruins of Manorbier Castle, where Giraldus Cambrensis (remembered

Chough

for the descriptions he made of his travels in Wales, Ireland and abroad) was born in 1147, are just a short distance from the path. Giraldus was a disappointed aspirant to the see of St David's and has left moving descriptions of the beauty and tranquillity of his ancestral home. The ruins, which may be visited, have been accounted the most perfect example extant of a Norman baron's residence (though Giraldus was half Welsh) with all the appurtenances of church, mill, dovecote, ponds and grove.

Just before reaching Manorbier Bay the path passes King's Quoit, a neolithic burial chamber (c3000BC); prehistoric remains are often found on little headlands such as this. We are now in an area where the rocks are of Old Red Sandstone. The path continues for eight miles along the cliffs past a whole series of beautiful sandy bays, Swanlake Bay, Freshwater East (where haphazard shack development is being tidied up) and thence by Stackpole Quay (see below), said to have the smallest quay in the country, to Stackpole Head and Broad Haven (see page 42). There are Iron Age camps on the east side of Freshwater East and at Greenala Point, and the cliffs in this area, now of limestone, provide further examples of caves and blowholes. There is no difficulty in finding one's way; the turf paths keep closely to the cliff edge.

At this point we are approaching the Castlemartin tank range. Times of firing are published locally and local information must be sought, though it will be found that the ranges are generally not in use on public holidays and summer weekends. When firing is not taking place the coast path may

Stackpole Quay on the south coast

The Pembrokeshire coast path at Broad Haven near Bosherston

be continued through the gate just beyond the car park on the west side of Broad Haven, and followed for about four miles to the limestone pillars of Elegug Stacks. This section of coast is of particular interest and grandeur and includes the viewpoint of St Govan's Head; St Govan's tiny, thirteenth-century stone chapel and holy well approached down a flight of steps cut in the rock (see opposite, top); several Iron Age forts on projecting headlands; and numerous caves, stacks, arches and blowholes (Bosherston Mere is the most remarkable) where the sea has cut or gouged out the limestone. It includes the ravine of Huntsman's Leap where the rider is said to have died of fright after clearing the abyss, and the fine natural arch of the Green Bridge of Wales. The cliffs and stacks are also particularly rich in bird-life and large colonies of guillemots, kittiwakes, razorbills and other sea-birds may be seen clinging to near-vertical faces, particularly at the western end.

The Angle Peninsula

If the way to St Govan's is closed there is a path leading from Broad Haven northwards to Bosherston. Bosherston Lakes have a fine show of water lilies in the summer. The main tank range at Castlemartin west of Elegug Stacks is not open at any time, so the fine cliffs between this point and Freshwater West cannot be visited at all. A detour must be made north and then west by road through Castlemartin village and the path picked up again just south of Broomhill Burrows to continue round the red sandstone cliffs of the Angle Peninsula to the village of Angle. The path along the south side of the peninsula was created for the long distance

St Govan's chapel at the foot of the
limestone cliffs on the south coast
(*Leonard and Marjory Gayton*)

Freshwater West looking south.
The path follows the line of dunes

path after a public inquiry in 1970. A fort built in 1854 against the fear of a French invasion guards the entrance to Milford Haven on Thorn Island, the counterpart of a similar fort across the water on the Dale Peninsula. East Blockhouse is also paired with West Blockhouse across the Haven, and quite a few other fortifications will be met with on the inner shores of the estuary, testifying to the importance then attached to the deep anchorage and the naval installations it gave rise to.

The path continues round Angle Bay (famous for cockles) to the first of the industrial sites opened in the early sixties. The BP crude oil terminal at Popton Point, opened in 1961, incorporates and makes use of a further nineteenth-century fort. The path then passes the Texaco refinery, opened in 1964, and the oil-fired power station at Pwllcrochan, and makes its way by an inland route to Pembroke. The castle, which dominates the town from a huge limestone rock in the river estuary and was the birth-place of Henry VII, was started by a Montgomery in 1090 and was completed in the thirteenth century by the Earls of Pembroke. The castle was sacked in 1648 by Cromwell, the defenders having recently changed over to the Royalist side. Three of the leading defenders were condemned to death, but it was later decided that only one should die and that he should be chosen by lot. The loser was Poyer, Mayor of Pembroke.

The Haven

From the industry of Pembroke Dock we cross the Haven by the new Cleddau bridge and are faced with further but more recent industrial landscapes—Neyland, the Gulf oil refinery, Milford Haven, Hakin, the Amoco refinery and the Esso refinery—to arrive at the quiet natural beauty of Sandy Haven. Here the river channel can only be crossed at low tide by a small footbridge; at other times an inland detour must be made because the bridge is submerged.

The edge of the red sandstone cliffs of the north side of the Haven and round the Dale Peninsula are followed to Dale Roads, past Dale Fort Field Studies Centre, and round St Ann's Head with its coastguard station and disused lighthouse. Henry VII landed in Mill Bay, near St Ann's Head, on 7 August 1485, before the Battle of Bosworth. Thence past the site of Dale Naval Airfield (now National Trust) to Marloes Sands, and round Wooltack Point to Deer Park, where there are defensive embankments across the peninsula dating from Iron Age times, but no deer. There are early Christian, Iron Age and earlier remains on both the south and north sides of the Marloes Peninsula and from Martinshaven sea trips may be arranged to view the colonies of sea-birds and seals which abound on this coast. A ferry also connects with Skomer Island which lies offshore and is a national nature reserve on account of the richness and variety of the bird-life which it supports.

The path continues to Musselwick Bay and The Nab (a Stone Age site for the manufacture of flint tools was discovered here), along contorted cliffs of red sandstone and grey cliffs of an earlier era, topped with windswept gorse, to the holiday resorts of Little Haven and Broad Haven. At Broad Haven is the Pembrokeshire Countryside Unit where information is available to the public about the national park and its natural history, and from which conducted walks along the coast path may be arranged.

St Brides Bay

From Little Haven to the top end of the long sweep of Newgale Sands the path runs along the low cliffs of St Brides Bay, with sandy reaches and caves below, using in part the coast road with its caravans and holiday bungalows. The darker rocks along St Brides Bay indicate the presence of the soft coal measures, of shales and sandstones, which have been eaten away to shape the bay itself, although older rocks also make their appearance near Druidston. The coal seams, which run out under the sea, were worked from the late Middle Ages and exported from Nolton Haven, and old shafts appear between here and Newgale. To seaward off Newgale, as in the area north of Saundersfoot, the fossilised stumps of a submerged prehistoric forest can be seen at low tides.

From Newgale onwards the path runs in an area which differs in character from what has gone before, an area of unspoilt rocky coast with fewer and smaller sandy inlets, a land of poor soil and scattered habitations, where the older and harder pre-Carboniferous rocks have been better able to resist the inroads of the sea. The people, more reserved in their manner, have maintained over the centuries their older way of life against the influences of Norman-English origin from the south of the county. Use of the Welsh language continues, as the placenames indicate; villages are smaller and more primitive and building styles more rugged and less colourful. Here too the evidence of the influence of the Celtic Church is more plentiful, reflecting the proximity to St David's.

Solva and St David's

Some three miles of cliff-top walking brings us to Solva, an attractive village in a narrow and steep-sided valley, in whose estuary many pleasure boats will be seen. It was a trading centre in the days when sea transport was the most natural way of supplying the hinterland. The path then continues along the richly coloured cliffs descending to tiny inlets where small streams meet the sea at Porth-y-rhaw and Caerbwdi where stone was taken to construct and repair the cathedral at St David's. From Caerfai Bay a road leads in half a mile to the city itself. St David's, 'the principal seat of Christianity in all the west' in the sixth century, has no more than 2,000 inhabitants. In 1120 St David's was raised by Pope Calixtus II to a holy place of pilgrimage where two visits were said to be worth one to St Peter's. Henry II visited it on his way to Ireland and one story has it that St Patrick started on his missionary voyage from here. The present structure, built inconspicuously in a hollow from reddish sandstone, was started in the twelfth century and not completed until 1522. The Bishop's Palace alongside was built about 1340 but abandoned in the eighteenth century and is now an impressive ruin.

There follows St Non's Bay with the tiny St Non's Chapel and the nearby holy well. (St Non was David's mother and the saint is said to have been born on the site of the chapel in the sixth century.) The long inlet of Porth-clais, once a small port, and Porthlysgi Bay, bring the walker to Ramsey Sound, whose swift currents separate the mainland from Ramsey Island. The island may be visited by boat from Porth Stinian near St Justinian's Chapel. It has prehistoric and early Christian remains and is interesting geologically, being comprised of igneous rocks in the north and sedimentary rocks of the Ordovician series in the south. It also has caves, the haunt of seals, and the high cliffs, outlying rocks and inlets

The Pembrokeshire coast path descending into Solva at the Gribin (*Leonard and Marjory Gayton*)

St David's Cathedral

are the nesting places of guillemots, razorbills, oyster-catchers and petrels, and more rarely falcons, buzzards and herons may be seen. The body of St Justinian, a colleague of St David, is said to have drifted from Ramsey Island, where he was martyred, to the site of the present roofless chapel, which was built in the early sixteenth century to replace the original structure.

The path then runs above Whitesand Bay with, at its northern end, St Patrick's Chapel, and on to St David's Head. St David's Head was known in classical times as Octopitarum Promontarium, a reference to rocks known as the Bishops and Clerks to the west of Ramsey Island. At that time this headland of jagged rock must have seemed to stand at one of the ends of the world. The area was no doubt known in those times to Etruscan and Carthaginian navigators venturing far from their Mediterranean homeland, and perhaps settled by earlier navigators who have left the remains of their settlement at the headland and at Carnllidi, the small conical hill overlooking it. Now it offers some of the grandest prospects of the whole route, its own wild and unspoilt beauty set off by the colours of the wild flowers that carpet it in spring and by purple heather in autumn.

The North Coast

The cliff path continues unbroken along the exposed and rugged coastline beneath Carnedd-lleithr and Penbiri, more rounded hills or 'monadnocks' that stand up above the Pembrokeshire plain, to Aber-Eiddy Bay. Here, at

Porthgain (less than three miles further on) and at Abercastell (five miles further still) there was slate working in the last century and, exceptionally, roads lead down to the coast. These roads lead from the coast to the small hamlets of Llanrhian, Trevine and, slightly more distant, to Mathry, and provide the opportunity of breaking the very long cliff-top journey between St David's Head and Strumble Head. There is a cromlech, Carreg Samson, just off the path along a farm lane (Long House) just before Abercastell is reached, and a hill fort at Pen Morfa beyond it. Further on towards Strumble Head prehistoric relics become more numerous and at Pwllderi there are hut circles on Garn-fawr hill with a hermit's 'bee-hive' hut just below. There is also a youth hostel at Pwllderi, which serves the long distance path.

Strumble Head, where there is a lighthouse, provides magnificent views from 400ft cliffs along the whole Welsh coast from St David's Head to Lleyn. Between the Head and Fishguard we pass St Degan's Chapel and at Carregwastad Point, in Aberfelin Bay, the site of the last invasion of Britain. Some 1,200 men landed from France in three frigates in 1797 under the command of the American Captain Tate, but were forced to surrender to the local yeomanry at Goodwick Sands.

East of Fishguard bold cliff-tops with fine views across Cardigan Bay are again followed to Dinas Island, in effect a peninsula, round which the path runs. The walker can also take the short cut across the neck of the peninsula to continue the journey to Newport Sands and the holiday town of Newport. There is also magnificent scenery in the final section of the coast path from Newport to St Dogmaels, culminating in the viewpoint of Cemaes Head. Numerous species of sea-birds, seals and many species of wild flowers may again be seen on this rugged and lonely shoreline.

5 · The South West Peninsula Coast Path

North Cornwall
Opened: 19 May 1973
Length: 137 miles (218km)

South Cornwall
Opened: 19 May 1973
Length: 133 miles (214km)

Dorset
Opened: 14 September 1974
Length: 72 miles (116km)

South Devon
Opened: 14 September 1974
Length: 93 miles (150km)

Somerset & North Devon
Opened:
Length: 82 miles (132km)

National Park Information Centres:

	Ordnance Survey Map Reference:
Minehead Market House, The Parade (Tel 2984)	SS 968 462
Lynmouth Parish Hall, Watermeet Road (Tel Lynton 2509)	SS 724 494
Combe Martin (caravan)—The Beach Car Park (Tel 3319)	SS 576 474

Thrift

A Long Coast Path

This very long path of 825km (515 miles) runs from Minehead in Somerset along the north coast of the peninsula, round Land's End, and back along the south coast to Studland in the Isle of Purbeck. It is in reality made up of five separate long distance paths begun at different times between 1952 and 1963. The earliest, the two Cornish paths, were opened in 1973 and the South Devon and Dorset Paths were opened in 1974; it is anticipated that the Somerset and North Devon Path will be opened soon.

Over such a long distance it is natural that a very great variety of scenery and conditions is to be encountered. In general the northern coastline is bold, rugged and high, its line being relatively little indented. The south coast is quiet, softer and deeply incised with attractive winding river valleys which penetrate far inland. These valleys were 'drowned' in post-glacial times so that the river mouths are now deep sea inlets. They are of very great natural beauty, but they also pose problems for the walker if, as sometimes happens, the ferry is irregular or no longer working. The path runs along the cliffs with splendid views of the sea, the rocks offering every conceivable variation of shape, colour and texture, headland succeeding headland in the view ahead, while inland there is a rich variety of changing landscapes as the different regions of the area are passed. The paths are punctuated by towns and villages, which are themselves rich in historic and other interest for the walker. A few are large, like Plymouth or Torquay, and some are holiday towns like Newquay, Sidmouth or St Ives, while many are small and quaint like Port Isaac, Mousehole or Polperro. These towns and villages divide the route into convenient sections, as starting and finishing points, and also provide accommodation. In general route-finding is not difficult as the paths follow the sea edge as closely as possible and, particularly near the holiday towns, are well trodden-out by visitors.

The *Somerset and North Devon Coast Path* of 130km (82 miles) runs from Minehead along the northern coastal boundary of the Exmoor National

Park, and through the North Devon area of outstanding natural beauty to the Cornwall county boundary about 11km (7 miles) beyond Hartland Point. It includes some of the most spectacular cliff and moorland scenery on the whole of the South West Peninsula Path, the high, rounded north-facing slopes of red sandstone falling sheer and smooth into the sea, while the west-facing slopes of grey slate further on extend jagged and broken edges seawards. With scarcely a break in the cliffs there is little room for towns, and Lynton and Combe Martin have to adapt themselves to the land available. The rolling moors of Exmoor are equally beautiful, whether bare or, as in the case of the narrow and precipitous valleys of the East and West Lyn, covered from top to bottom with great cascades of woodland. Further west there is more room. The path runs near to the historic, seafaring towns of Barnstaple, Bideford and Appledore, and takes in the duneland of Braunton Burrows and the smooth line of almost inaccessible coast of folded dark rocks in Bideford Bay.

The Route: Minehead and Exmoor

The coast path starts above the harbour in Minehead at North Hill, passing through Culver Cliff Wood to join the metalled track which runs westwards along a ridge set back from the sea but with sea views. The cliff edge is heavily wooded and cut by steep ravines. The 'hog's-back' cliffs of hard Devonian rocks at this point are typical of those to be met with along the coast westwards as far as Combe Martin, and their shape determines to a large extent the line taken by the path. The land, instead of forming an

North Devon and Somerset section of the south-west path looking eastwards along the coast to Little Hangman and Great Hangman

Culbone Church

abrupt high edge at the sea, falls smoothly but very steeply seawards, the steepness often increasing as the land descends. It would be perilous to walk on the lower falling ground where in any case there is often dense vegetation or woodland, and the path generally runs high up on the ridge. The path climbs almost to the 1,000ft summit of Selworthy Beacon below which is Selworthy, said to be the most beautiful village in England. The path then takes us round Hurtstone Point or, as an alternative, we can take the easier attractive route round the back of the headland down Hurtstone Combe below Bossington Hill, before dropping down into Bossington. Porlock lies in the agricultural plain and marshland the sea edge of which we can follow to Porlock Weir. There are views across to the Welsh coast twelve miles away.

The path climbs steeply through Yearnor Wood to Culbone, a few houses with a tiny church (see left), one of several that claim to be the smallest in England; it was in a farmhouse near Culbone that Coleridge wrote *Kubla Khan*. We skirt several wooded combes (the coast is very heavily wooded here) by Silcombe, Broomstreet and Yenworthy to Cosgate Hill on the south side of the busy A39 road, leaving out Old Barrow Hill, and at White Gate follow the fence down to join the old low-level path well down the cliff side. This path leads to the access road to Foreland Lighthouse, and it is possible to go right down to the lighthouse and along the western side of the Foreland, but the narrow track is on a precipitous slope which plunges down to the sea far below and in a high wind it could be dangerous. The walker should therefore cut across the headland to the great rocky ravine of Great Red. It is then a magnificent walk around the cliffs well above sea-level, nearly into Countisbury and thence to the A39, where the path follows first the south and then the north side of the road and down steeply into Lynmouth.

The whole area covered by the path so far is within the Exmoor National Park. Inland the scenery is no less striking than the view seawards, of open moor or wooded valley. At Cosgate Hill, look down to Oare Water, towards Brendon and Malmsmead, and recall the exploits of *Lorna Doone*. At Lynmouth it is a short walk to the splendours of Watersmeet where Hoaroak Water plunges precipitously into the quieter waters of the East Lyn.

On from Lynton

West of Lynton the path takes the town walks overlooking the sea round Hollerday Hill to the crags of the Valley of the Rocks, and the sandstone block of Castle Hill. The old toll road from the Valley of the Rocks leads past Lee Bay to Woody Bay where the sea has eroded the softer slates and trees have filled the sheltered bays. The route does not go down to Woody Bay (to which a narrow road leads from Inkerman Bridge), but follows a road parallel to and well above the shoreline to a sharp bend. At this point a gate leads on to the broad track of the old coach road which continues at uniform height above the sea to Heddon's Mouth and up the deep wooded ravine in which flows the River Heddon to Hunter's Inn where there is opportunity for refreshment.

From Trentishoe it is intended that the path should double back to the cliff on the seaward side of the fields and across Trentishoe and Holdstone Downs and thence round or across the deep gash at Sherrycombe to Great Hangman. If rights of way are not yet available roads at some distance from the coast can be followed. From Little Hangman there is a much-used path down to Combe Martin, where the town, having no room to expand along the coast, stretches back as ribbon development up its valley. After Combe Martin the A399 runs close to the coastline but the path avoids it as much as possible, using the seaward side where it can, passing Watermouth Caves, the Victorian castle of Watermouth and a large caravan site, to Hele Bay and Ilfracombe. West of Ilfracombe the Torrs Walks lead to Lee Bay at the end of a superb wooded valley, continuing to the lighthouse at Bull Point and to Morte Point where the sharp rocks have caused many shipwrecks. From Woolacombe Sands the path goes through the dunes from the beach car park to Puttsborough Village, then by the path round Baggy Point to Croyde Bay. Colonies of sea-birds may be observed round the Point, as well as the occasional seal. The road which follows the shoreline may be used to Saunton Sands Hotel and Braunton Burrows but a projected path just off the road may be provided later. Braunton Burrows covers an area of about two square miles. Parts of it have been made a nature reserve because of its botanical interest, and nature trails have been laid out. Extensive marshlands have developed behind the dunes. The path enters the town of Braunton, technically a village, the largest in England, by Braunton Great Field, a rare survival from the medieval agricultural system of strip cultivation.

The Taw and the Torridge

The break in the path due to the Taw and Torridge estuaries must be negotiated by road and the route picked up again at Westward Ho! Westward Ho! was named after Kipling's novel in 1863 when an important new settlement was to be developed, but the ambitious plans came to little. Kipling was educated in the original village in a college (later transferred elsewhere) that formed the basis for *Stalky & Co*. The ferry across the Torridge from Instow to the picturesque village of Appledore, where there are two famous shipyards, one using traditional craft methods and the other building steel ships by the most up-to-date methods, shortens the journey across the Torridge. But there is no such convenient way across the Taw.

The extensive beaches of Saunton Sands north of the estuaries, and of Westward Ho! Sands south of them, where the sea comes rolling in with great breakers, as well as the equally extensive dunes at Braunton Burrows and Northam Burrows, are impressive, particularly when seen without the holiday crowds which gather here in the summer. Together both beaches extend for five miles. The whole area of the estuaries, with Barnstaple and Bideford not far away, is steeped in seafaring history.

The coastline swings away from Westward Ho! along Abbotsham Cliffs in the great loop of Barnstaple Bay, at the other end of which is Hartland Point. The cliffs of dark shale and sandstone of the Carboniferous period are low (though they get higher as one goes west, particularly near Hartland Point) and form one long smooth sweep with no natural bays, and therefore no harbours. Numerous short streams have, however, cut deep and wooded hanging valleys as at Peppercombe, Bucks Mills, Clovelly and Mouthmill and these form waterfalls at the coastline. The reason is that the coast is being eroded so rapidly that the streams have not the time to cut their beds down to sea-level. There are paths along the coastline but there is no continuous right of way at present along the

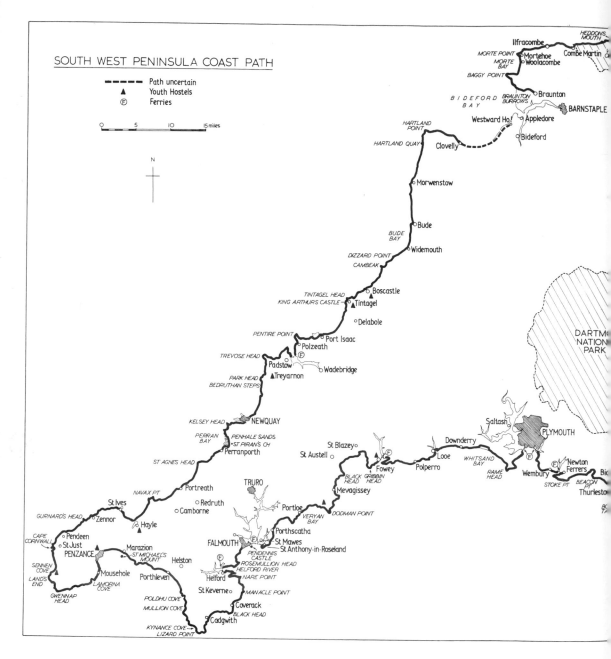

SOUTH WEST PENINSULA COAST PATH

- - - - Path uncertain
▲ Youth Hostels
Ⓕ Ferries

0   5   10   15 miles

N

HEDDONS MOUTH
Ilfracombe
MORTE POINT Mortehoe
MORTE BAY Woolacombe Combe Martin
BAGGY POINT
BIDEFORD BAY *BRAUNTON BURROWS* Braunton
BARNSTAPLE
Westward Ho! Appledore
HARTLAND POINT Bideford
HARTLAND QUAY Clovelly
Morwenstow
Bude
BUDE BAY
DIZZARD POINT Widemouth
CAMBEAK
TINTAGEL HEAD Boscastle
KING ARTHURS CASTLE ▲Tintagel
Delabole
PENTIRE POINT Port Isaac
TREVOSE HEAD Polzeath
Padstow Ⓕ
Wadebridge
PARK HEAD ▲Treyarnon
BEDRUTHAN STEPS
KELSEY HEAD NEWQUAY
PERRAN BAY *PENHALE SANDS*
ST PIRAN'S CH
Perranporth
ST AGNES HEAD
Portreath
NAVAX PT Redruth
St Ives Camborne
GURNARD'S HEAD Zennor
CAPE CORNWALL Pendeen Hayle
St Just TRURO
PENZANCE Marazion
ST MICHAEL'S MOUNT Helston
Mousehole Porthleven
SENNEN COVE
LAND'S END *LAMORNA COVE*
GWENNAP HEAD St Keverne
POLDHU COVE
MULLION COVE Coverack
BLACK HEAD
KYNANCE COVE Cadgwith
LIZARD POINT
Helford
MANACLE POINT
NARE POINT
FALMOUTH Ⓕ
PENDENNIS CASTLE
ROSEMULLION HEAD
HELFORD RIVER
St Mawes
St Anthony-in-Roseland
Portscatha
VERYAN BAY
Portloe
DODMAN POINT
Mevagissey
Portloe
St Austell *BLACK GRIBBIN HEAD*
St Blazey Fowey Ⓕ
Polperro
Looe
Downderry
WHITSAND BAY
RAME HEAD
Wembury
STOKE PT
Saltash
PLYMOUTH Ⓕ
Newton Ferrers Ⓕ
BEACON PT
Thurleston
DARTMOOR NATIONAL PARK

whole length to Mouthmill. There are, however, roads down to
Peppercombe, Buck's Mills and Clovelly, from which the coastline can be
appreciated. Up-to-date information about access along the coast should
be sought locally. The picturesqueness of Clovelly, its steep, cobbled street
with no cars, and its charming houses, is well known. Access to and from
Clovelly to the east is available along the Hobby Drive almost as far as
Buck's Mills, to cars as well as pedestrians, and from here the sweep of the
coastline can be seen.

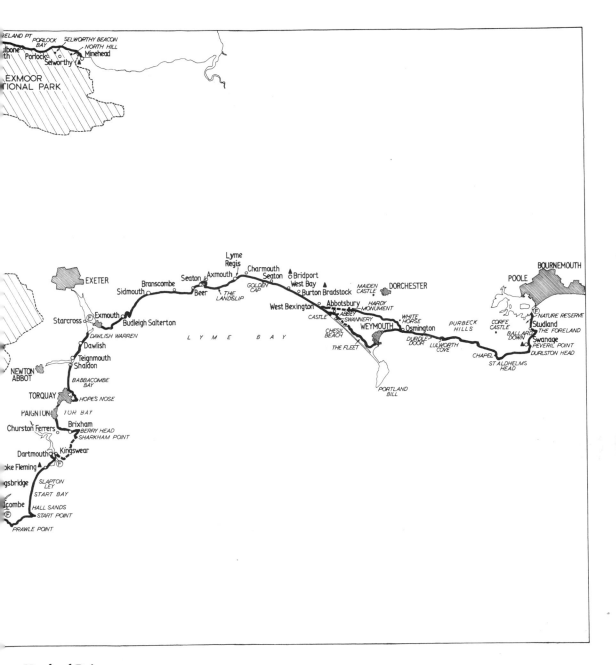

Hartland Point

An area belonging to the services is fenced off just before reaching
Hartland Point (though coastal access may soon be permitted), where
there is a lighthouse, built in 1874, on a lower promontory standing out
from the Point. From the Point there are magnificent views, with Morte
Point to the east, Trevose Head to the west and the Welsh coast far away
on the horizon. The coast and the path now change direction to run due
south, past the Cow and Calf rocks, along vertical cliffs in highly folded

and contorted rocks with jagged edges running out to sea where the harder rock has resisted erosion and the softer rocks have been eaten away, forming caves in some places. These savage rocks are notorious for the shipwrecks they have caused at times of onshore winds. Almost every stream ends in a waterfall (the best known is at Speke's Mill Mouth), often stepped where it flows successively over harder and softer rocks.

At Hartland Quay, two miles south of the Point, the quay has long disappeared. The first one, built by the monks of Hartland Abbey, a mile inland along one of the larger valleys and now replaced by an eighteenth-century building, was improved in 1566 under a Bill sponsored by Sir Walter Raleigh, Sir Francis Drake and Sir John Hawkins, and finally washed away at the end of the last century. The eighteenth-century mansion which incorporates parts of the original abbey may be visited at times advertised locally.

The *Cornwall North Coast Path* is 216km (135 miles) long and continues the route along a bleak and inhospitable coast of sharp rocks that has seen many shipwrecks, past Bude, Boscastle and Tintagel to Padstow and the Camel estuary. After Trevose Head there are sandy bays and long stretches of beach against which great Atlantic rollers break majestically to Newquay and the Camel estuary and to Perranporth. The coast reverts to its rugged character round St Agnes Head to Godrevy Point and the huge areas of blown sand in St Ives Bay. Between St Ives Bay and Mounts Bay the rocks change their character and the hard granite mass of the St Just peninsula is almost cut off from the rest of Cornwall where these two bays almost meet across the peninsula. This bleak coast is bold, wild and treeless, the fields are small, the stone houses with their slate roofs standing squat and square against the wind. Tin-mining has been a traditional industry from very early times in this ancient Celtic land of saints and legends, and has somehow woven itself into the mystique of the area. Active workings, and the near-romantic ruins of abandoned mines, will be seen along the path, which ends at Penzance.

The Route: To Beyond Bude

This part of the South West Peninsula Path begins at the Combe of Marsland Mouth, which marks the county boundary with Devon. Some of the sailors wrecked on this coast are buried in the churchyard at Morwenstow, between 1834 and 1875 the living of the Rev Stephen Hawker, poet and prototype of nineteenth-century eccentrics. It was he who wrote the well-known refrain 'And shall Trelawney die?' and started the custom of harvest festivals. The hut on the cliffs, built from the wood of shipwrecked vessels, which he used as his retreat can be easily visited from the path. The isolated church (see left), and also the odd Gothic vicarage he had built, are worth the slight detour to see. A mile and a half to the south along the clearly defined cliff-top track the path passes the seaward edge of the former Cleave Camp where the military huts have been replaced by the dishes and other equipment of a satellite tracking station.

The holiday resort of Bude has attractive stretches of sandy beach and downland, and the canal, now derelict, is of some interest. Extending for thirty miles to Launceston it was built in 1819–26 and carried large quantities of sand from the beach for use as fertiliser because of its high lime content. From Bude southwards there is a road which keeps close to

Morwenstow Church

the coast to beyond Widemouth; this area is crowded in the summer with holiday-makers who are attracted to Widemouth Beach, and there is much modern development. The path follows the cliff with its twisted and broken rock strata but also uses the road for short sections. Past Millook the path comes to an extensive area at Dizzard Point which is prone to landslides, and the cliff path runs back from the sea and reaches Crackington Haven, popular for its surfing and bathing.

Less than a mile further on the path comes to the viewpoint at Cambeak, then past more land-slipping to Rusey Cliff and Beeny Cliff and on to Pentorgon Beach, where there is a waterfall, and into Boscastle. Boscastle Harbour is squeezed in a narrow ravine and the setting is as picturesque as the coast, where the sea and river waters meet, is wild. There is an interesting Witches Museum in the village. West of Boscastle on Forrabury Common a further survival of the ancient strip system of farming may be seen.

Bossiney Bay is a pleasant little inlet close to Willapark, a peninsula almost severed from the land, like Tintagel, offering an ideal defensive site for the Iron Age men who built the hillfort there. Sir Francis Drake was one of the two MPs sent to Parliament from Bossiney. A walk off the route up Rocky Valley would bring one to St Nectan's Kieve, where there is a forty-foot waterfall and an ancient hermitage.

Tintagel

It was Geoffrey of Monmouth, writing in the twelfth century, who first wreathed Tintagel in an air of romantic mystery associated with King Arthur, and the castle and monastery ruins on the 'island', which is in fact a peninsula where the connecting neck has partly collapsed, has become a place of pilgrimage for thousands of tourists. The present castle was built in the twelfth century by an Earl of Cornwall, but the earlier associations of the site were taken up and elaborated by Tennyson. King Arthur, the legendary defender of the Britons against the Saxons, is said to have been born here after Uther, then King of the Britons, introduced himself with Merlin's help into an earlier castle, where the Earl of Cornwall had hidden his wife Ygranie. The way from the village to the castle ruins, which are impressive as much for their wild and romantic setting and their caves as for the ruins themselves, is by a steep track, and in summer there is a private minibus service which operates at some inconvenience to those who prefer to walk. Seaward of these ruins are the even more interesting remains of a Celtic monastery dating perhaps from the sixth century where the outlines of the cells of the hermit monks may still be seen and will stimulate speculation about the men who chose such an austere but beautiful site to exercise their piety. The village of Tintagel has commercialised its historical assets and there is a good trade in mementoes of the Knights of the Round Table; but the quaint old post office, formerly a manor house and now owned by the National Trust, is worth visiting.

The path continues along the cliffs which are still punctuated by little streams pouring down their tiny valleys into the sea, and necessitating frequent ascents and descents, past the remains of the Treligga war-time encampment to Portgaverne and Port Isaac. Port Isaac is one of many attractive villages on the north coast of Cornwall, with narrow streets and alleys and colour-washed houses piled one on top of the other within a narrow combe. The old part of the village is around the harbour where fishermen still congregate. There is a right of way round the next headland to Pine Haven but none at present for the next two miles of coast, and an inland path must be used from the top of the ravine which opens into the Haven, across to Portquin. Portquin is no more than a cluster of old houses in a tiny but beautiful bay. Doyden Castle is a folly built in 1830.

The Camel Estuary and Newquay

Rumps Point, which has a prehistoric encampment and caves, and Pentire Point provide specially good and all-embracing views over the sea, including, in the case of the latter, views across Padstow Bay to Stepper Point which the path will reach shortly. But first there are the holiday sands of Hayle Bay before one reaches the open and beautiful Camel estuary which is followed inland past Brea Hill to the ferry for Padstow, which leaves from the sailing centre of Rock. The Camel estuary with its banks of sands is a most beautiful and lonely area and a haunt of water-birds; now that a footpath has been opened along the abandoned railway line on the south bank there is access to the whole estuary between Wadebridge and Padstow. Padstow is another distinctively Cornish small town. Founded by St Petroc, who crossed from Ireland in the sixth century and built a monastery, it has narrow streets, old stone buildings and interesting activity going on round the harbour. The harbour is a refuge for sailors travelling along this dangerous coast, which has seen many shipwrecks, though entry to the estuary is impeded by the 'Doom Bar'. Each year on May Day the ancient 'Hobby Horse Day' dance takes place in Padstow's streets.

The walk from Padstow north along the west side of the Camel estuary and around Stepper Point is exceptionally fine with great banks of sand at Hawkers Cove and magnificent views at the Point. Westwards there is a series of fine bays which are thronged on fine days in summer by visitors, who particularly appreciate the surfing on the great Atlantic rollers. The tiny Trevone and Harlyn bays are on the east side of the Trevose peninsula, where again there are exceptional sea views round the whole horizon. In 1900 some 150 skeletons were unearthed at Harlyn Bay together with Iron Age implements and other evidence of a thriving community; there is a small museum exhibiting the finds. On the west side of the peninsula is the magnificent Constantine Bay, and the smaller Treyarnon and Porthcothan bays, but the natural beauty of these bays is best appreciated outside the holiday season. South of Porthcothan are the much photographed Bedruthan Steps, the steps being originally the giant rocks on the beach which were stepping stones for a Cornish giant called Bedruthan. The ordinary steps down to the beach, closed until recently, have now been re-opened. The fine series of beaches round the Point are continued in Mawgan Porth and Watergate Beach which are easily accessible by road and very popular. There are many caves in this area where the soft shale has been eaten away. These fine westward-facing beaches are also very suitable for surfing and those which extend in front of Newquay and to the back of it round Towan Head have made Newquay perhaps the most popular holiday resort in Cornwall; and it has every attraction for the visitor. Last century it was important for fishing, and the Huer's House may still be seen on the headland near the harbour. The Huer's job was to raise the hue and cry when he sighted pilchards.

From the Gannel to St Ives

Crossing the Gannel estuary from East Pentire to Crantock may cause problems out of the holiday season. The channel through the sands is deep but it may be crossed by a footbridge at very low tide. In the summer months a ferry service is operated. From Penpol Creek on the south side of the Gannel, also crossed by a small plank bridge at its head, the path continues round Pentire Point West and Kelsey Head, which has an Iron Age promontory fort, to Holywell Beach and Holywell (the holy well in question is in a cave above the beach). Penhale Sands is taken up by a military firing range and the route takes a south-east course along a narrow road from Holywell, and curves south round the inland side of the sands for 1½ miles before taking a north-west course between Gear Sands and Penhale Sands, past St Piran's Church, to the edge of the dunes and into the former miners' town of Perranporth, now a holiday resort noted for its surfing. The seventh-century church was overwhelmed by sand in the eleventh century and dug out in the nineteenth, and is now protected from further encroachment by a concrete wall. The remains of a church built when the earlier one disappeared in the sand, and a 9ft Celtic cross, are nearby. St Piran was one of the numerous saints who sailed from Ireland in the sixth and seventh centuries, in his case on a millstone

The coast path at Clodgy Point, west of St Ives (*E W Tattersall*)

(possibly an allusion to the circular altar stones in use at the time, which he may have brought over). He is the patron saint of tinners.

From Perranporth to the viewpoint at St Agnes Head, crowned with heather, gorse and sea pinks, there is much evidence of tin-working and many old mine shafts, for here igneous rocks begin to intrude among the slates to form the metal-bearing veins. Some of the caves at Droskyn Point, overlooking Perranporth, may have been made artificially in the course of early workings. Before the Head is reached the path passes Trevaunance Cove, where the configuration and setting of the land compose an attractive picture in the blues, yellows, greens and browns of sea, sand, land and rocks. South of St Agnes Head, particularly past Portreath, coast erosion has given rise to frequent stacks and islands in the soft slates—Gull Rock, Samphire Island and Crane Island—and the sandy inlets at Chapel Porth and Porth Cowan are very beautiful. Onwards from Portreath the cliffs at Carvannel and Reskajeage Downs and at Hudder Down are within reach of the nearby road and are well known, Deadman's Cove and Hell's Mouth, where the sea comes crashing among the jagged rocks, being of particular interest. Some two miles inland are the industrial twin towns of Camborne–Redruth, the centre of the Cornish tin-mining industry and famous for the School of Mining at Camborne.

From the headland with the two points of Navax and Godrevy the view opens out across St Ives Bay towards St Ives Point and St Ives. The path proceeds along Gwithian and Upton Towans to the ferry at Hayle Towans but some walkers prefer to use the beach, which has been formed by accumulations of blown sand, rather than follow the cliff-top. Difficulty has been experienced in finding the ferry service working and since this stretch of urban and industrial landscape is one of the less attractive sections of the route some prefer simply to proceed directly by road to St Ives. The holiday town of St Ives was once a considerable port, pilchards, copper and tin being the main exports, but it has succeeded in maintaining its old-world character, particularly in the steep, narrow streets on the strip of land forming The Island, which divides its two beaches. Since the end of the last century it has become a centre for artists and many well-known painters have settled there, attracted by the climate, the scenery and the light.

The Penwith Peninsula

The coast from St Ives westwards to Land's End has a strong claim to being considered the finest stretch of cliff scenery of all, and its attractiveness is enhanced by its great length and the wildness and interest of the surrounding country. It is a landscape of rugged headlands, where Atlantic breakers crash ceaselessly against unyielding rocks, of tiny wind-swept fields and stone walls, and almost entirely without trees. The going may be rough where undergrowth has encroached on the path, and west of St Ives towards and beyond Clodgy Point the ground is broken and marshy and requires some care in picking one's way. Halfway to Pendeen the grey, stone village of Zennor deserves a slight detour (in addition to the church and a good example of a cromlech there is a small museum), and there is an optional path round Gurnard's Head, which juts far out into the sea. Gurnard's Head is the site of an exceptionally strong hill-fort, and is a viewing platform for the whole of this exceptional coast. This is

Engine house in the heart of the tin-mining country

also the heart of the tin-mining country, and miners' cottages, mine shafts, hoisting gear, engine houses and stone chimney stacks are dotted about the countryside, particularly near the coast, for workings went far out to sea. Between Pendeen and St Just the signs of mining activity increase dramatically. The Geevor mine is still working, and the sea is coloured brown where one passes along the cliffs in front of the untidy paraphernalia of débris of a working mine. Great local pride is felt for the achievements of the miners who produced great wealth in the heyday of the industry before more easily won tin was discovered in Malaya and elsewhere, and there is great affection for the engine houses and other relics of this era. West Cornwall was also the last stronghold of the Cornish language.

The path continues to the headland of Pendeen Watch, where there is a lighthouse, and to Cape Cornwall, and from there along the cliffs to Whitesand Bay, with the scattered modern village of Sennen Cove at its southern end, and thence to the columnar rock formations of Land's End. Sennen is reputed to have been the site of a land battle, in which King Arthur was victorious over Norse invaders of Cornwall. Land's End is much visited and has a café; the Longships Lighthouse can be seen offshore. There are further granite outposts at Gwennap Head and Cribba Head where the scenery is no less dramatic than at the more popular Land's End. Fast-flowing streams have cut narrow channels in the coastline to Lamorna Cove, where the main granite strata end and the greenstone begins.

Nanjizal, south-east of Land's End

Mousehole, a quaint old fishing village which was sacked by the Spaniards in 1595 and where the last native speaker of Cornish died in 1777, is followed by picturesque Newlyn, beyond which there is a huge quarry producing a very hard type of roadstone. We are now on the road into Penzance, which is the end of the north coast route.

The *Cornwall South Coast Path* of 214km (133 miles) curves from Penzance round the low edge of Mount's Bay past a number of small bays to the Lizard peninsula. Here, as in the St Just peninsula, granite and granite-like rock has resisted erosion, but the Helford River has eaten into its soft northern flank, half-isolating it from the rest of Cornwall. At Carrick Roads the vast mouth of a drowned river valley breaks the continuity of the shoreline. There follows Veryan Bay and St Austell Bay behind which rise the spoil heaps of china-clay workings. At Fowey another drowned river valley with beautiful sheltered banks and forgotten side-creeks again breaks the coastline and the path begins a wide sweep along low cliffs, which takes it eventually to Rame Head, Penlee Point and Plymouth Sound.

The Route: Penzance to Prussia Cove

The path begins east of Penzance, where the main railway line and the main road hug the coast as far as Marazion and force the path on to a narrow strip above the sands. St Michael's Mount is a granite outlier where the romantically sited modern castle is built on the site of a Benedictine priory. It is approachable at low tide by a causeway from Marazion, where Jewish settlers in the Middle Ages traded in tin, and is open to the public at advertised times.

Along the low, sandy cliffs to the east further headlands jut into Mount's Bay at Cudden Point (which is of greenstone) and at Rinsey Head, Hoe Point and Trewards Head (which are of granite) with the long line of Prah Sands lying between the first two of these latter headlands. There are several pleasant coves at Cudden Point, the best known being Prussia Cove, named after the 'King of Prussia', leader of an eighteenth-century band of smugglers. At Porthleven is the beginning of the Lizard peninsula and at Looe Pool the strong currents sweeping round the bay have built a storm beach, or barrier of shingle, damming the natural outlet of the river coming down from Helston and forming a lake. This bar had previously to be cut to allow the water to escape but there is now a culvert under the shingle.

The Lizard

The cliff path down the Lizard Point is marked by a number of small and extremely attractive coves—Poldhu Cove, Polurrian Cove, Mullion Cove and Kynance Cove among others. The latter two are particularly beautiful and possess an extraordinary wealth of features of natural interest, caves, arches and rocky crevices, colourful cliffs and a particularly fine and light sand deriving from the serpentine rock. Poldhu achieved fame when it became the site of Marconi's experiments in wireless telegraphy in 1901, and an obelisk marks the place from which the transmissions to Newfoundland were made. Apart from the sharp descents and ascents at the coves the cliff-top is flat and the characteristic rock is the beautiful serpentine, much used for the local carving of souvenirs, which may be well seen on both sides of Lizard Point, the most southerly part of

Coverack Harbour, Cornwall
(*E W Tattersall*)

England and the site of a lighthouse. The wild contorted cliffs continue beyond the Point but here they are lower and less dramatic, though hardly less beautiful, and the path drops down to the small fishing village of Cadgwith, where there are attractive houses of stone and thatch. Just south of the village is the Devil's Frying Pan, a deep funnel in the rock 200ft deep.

The path rounds the serpentine headlands of Nare Point and Chynhall Point, past more small coves, to Coverack, a somewhat larger village also with stone and thatch houses. Nare Point opens up views of the Helford River and to Rosemullion across the Helford estuary. The serpentine is a sedimentary rock, magnesian limestone, which has been metamorphosed by heat and pressure and often mixed with other minerals. When it is polished one is able to look, as it were, into the mineral and observe a variety of forms and colours. At Chynhall Point there is an Iron Age camp. But north of Coverack and before Chynhall Point and Nare Point are reached the coastal area is much affected by quarrying and the path takes a quarry road inland from Dean Point to Rosenithon, Porthoustock, Trenance and Porthallow, where it reverts to the cliff-top. Round Nare Point comes Gillan Creek where it should be possible to arrange a crossing direct to St Anthony. There is a path round Dennis Point, but the coast on the south side of the Helford River in front of Bosahan House is not available and the Manaccan road must be taken to the ferry point across the estuary at Helford. Helford, pressed into the head of a narrow valley, has thatched roofs, trees and flowers and many boats and yachtsmen.

The Helford River

We are now in an area which is scenically more subdued than the rugged west of Cornwall we have just left, and the Helford River with its lazy creeks is representative of the quiet charm and serene beauty to be met with later in other drowned valleys along the south coast of the peninsula. This is true also of the north shore of the estuary (both are sheltered from the prevailing west winds) past Mawnan to Rosemullion Head and Falmouth, the cliffs being noticeably gentler and less awesome in aspect.

A scheduled ferry service runs from Falmouth to the elegant and fashionable town of St Mawes, but the further crossing from St Mawes to the beach at St Anthony in Roseland is less certain and local information should be sought. On the way across to St Mawes the ferry passes under St Mawes Castle, a well-maintained fortification built for Henry VIII, 1540–43, to guard the entrance to Carrick Roads, and matched by Pendennis Castle on the Falmouth side. From St Anthony Head at the bottom of the Roseland Peninsula the path goes north to Porthmellin Head and Greeb Point, with extensive views across Gerrans Bay, and into Porthscatho and on to Pendower Beach and Nare Head itself. The view from Nare Head stretches across the wide curve of Veryan Bay to the Dodman, and the path is along low, lonely cliffs through the tiny, half-forgotten coast villages of Portloe and Portholland and past the modern mansion of Caerhays Castle at the rear of the fine sands of Porthluney Cove. On gorse-covered Dodman is a promontory fort and a cross erected as a landmark for sailors, and from it there are spectacular views in both directions.

After Gorran Haven, which has attractive slate-hung cottages, come Maenease Point and Chapel Point, followed by Porthmellin and Mevagissey. This latter small town has kept some of its old-world charm as a fishing port. Its prosperity was based on pilchards and it has managed to preserve its fisheries as a live industry. At Pentewan there is a large caravan camp facing the sands and the path must follow the road behind. Black Head is another narrow-necked promontory with a prehistoric settlement and is the counterpart to Chapel Point across Mevagissey Bay. Beyond it we continue to the quiet charm of Trenarren village, and along the coast to Porthpean.

China Clay

We are now in the area of the china clay industry of which St Austell is the thriving capital, and Charlestown is its busy port. Kaolin, or china clay, was formed by gases from the interior of the earth which decomposed the granite into its natural constituents. Water pressure is applied to wash out the clay and the slurry is left to settle in tanks where the clay can be dug out when it is dry. The other constituents, quartz and mica, form the eerie conical white waste tips which are seen far and wide in the area. Economic use of these tips, or at least their assimilation into the landscape poses a problem; projects to fabricate building blocks from the material have suffered from the high cost of transport. The china clay is used in the manufacture of many unsuspected materials—paper, rubber, paint, plastics and insecticides. East of Charlestown are Par Sands where the effects of the china clay working are evident, and even the sea is discoloured by the white effluent.

The coastline now veers due south towards the slate cliffs of Gribbin Head, but first leads to the sheltered harbour and hamlet of Polkerris, a gem spot of a few houses which has an interesting inn full of all kinds of curiosities including firearms and brasses. From Gribbin Head, surmounted by a beacon painted in red and white bands, there are views across St Austell Bay in one direction and away as far as Rame Head on the other. Round the Head and up a wooded valley are the gardens and exotic trees of Menabilly House, once the home of the Rashleigh family, which has been prominent in the Fowey area since the sixteenth century, but now associated with the du Mauriers. In the cliffs at the bottom of this valley is a grotto richly decorated with shells. Further on the way to Fowey we pass the ruins of St Catherine's Castle and soon come to Readymoney Bay and the town.

Fowey to Plymouth Sound

Fowey is an old-world place with a difference. It is commercially important as a port for the export of china clay, and foreign sailors may be encountered in its narrow and crooked streets. Hemmed in along the shores of a beautiful estuary it has, in fact, a curiously foreign air, possibly due to its long associations with France since the Middle Ages. In 1347 the town sent forty-seven ships and 700 men to the Siege of Calais, and it was sacked by the French in 1457. There is a ferry across to Polruan on the opposite bank, from where wild and rocky cliffs lead to Lantic Bay and Lantivet on a beautiful section of coast. Polperro, a postcard village, has become commercialised and is much visited by tourists, but round the harbour it has not yet lost its former character. From Polperro to Looe there is a well-used path along cliffs of green slate. Looe, built on both sides of a steep-sided and deep gorge, is also a tourist centre, but has its share of quaint streets and picturesque corners.

From East Looe the path starts well inland since cliff falls have destroyed the path along the sea front, and passes through a residential area to Millendreath Beach and thence, below Bodigga, Windsworth and Murrayton Farms, over rough overgrown ground made by old landslips, to Seaton. From Seaton the path eastwards to Downderry is along the beach, or the road may be followed. In any case the road must be joined at Downderry for a short way, and thence along Batten and Eglarooze Cliffs to the cluster of houses making up the hamlet of Portwrinkle. At Long Sands the road inland must be followed because of a rifle range, and although the route returns to the coast it is now road walking, or walking just off the military road wherever there is an open verge, almost the whole way to Rame Head, reverting to footpath from there to Penlee Point; and thence by footpath through the woods to Cawsand and Kingsand and round the seaward edge of Mount Edgcumbe Park. This is the former home of Lord Mount Edgcumbe, but is now owned jointly by Plymouth Corporation and Cornwall County Council. The extensive grounds are open to the public as a country park. The mansion had the strange misfortune, bearing in mind its isolated situation, of being severely damaged by bombs during the war. The ferry from Cremyll leads to Plymouth.

A feature of the *Devon South Coast Path* of 150km (93 miles) is the succession of estuaries on drowned river valleys that break up the low cliff line—the Yealm, the Erme, the Avon, Salcombe Harbour, the Dart and the Teign, all of them extremely beautiful, the wooded Dart Valley being quite outstanding. This phenomenon is due, as in Cornwall, to the raising of the sea level at the end of the Ice Age when the sea entered and found its natural level inland. One effect of these long valleys has been to restrict east–west communications, the main roads tending to run inland where the rivers are narrower and can be bridged (though the Teign has been bridged at its mouth). The result is that the coast near these broad estuaries, on one side if not on both, has been isolated, and remains remote and relatively natural and untouched by development. From Bolt Tail to Bolt Head and across Salcombe Harbour to Prawle Point and Start Point hard rock has resisted sea erosion and the whole area projects seaward in a great mass of rugged headlands and steep cliffs. From Brixham northwards a succession of towns crowds along the coast—Paignton, Torquay,

Looking west from Weston Mouth, Branscombe, on the South Devon section of the path

Teignmouth and Dawlish. There is interesting undeveloped coast between some of these towns, of which the path takes advantage, but its continuity is broken over this section. East of the estuary of the Exe is a long stretch of subdued and attractive coastal landscape to Seaton in which lie the holiday towns of Exmouth, Budleigh Salterton and Sidmouth. Here the colour of the soil and cliffs has changed dramatically to the bright red of the New Red Sandstone so closely associated with Devon. Eastward of Seaton is the Axmouth Landslip.

The Route: Turnchapel to Salcombe

The coast path begins at Turnchapel on the east side of Plymouth Sound and follows the road past Stamford Fort, leaving it where it curves round to Staddon Fort to make for Staddon Point and the series of small bays—Bovisand, Crownhill and Heybrook—which lie between Staddon Heights and Wembury Point. There are views across the Sound with the massive breakwater in the foreground, a mile long and completed in 1841 by John Rennie to provide a safe anchorage, but the coast, though still attractive, is still within the influence of Plymouth and apart from the nineteenth-century forts there are services training areas and aerial masts for long-range communication. There are also holiday caravans and bungalows in the shelter of the bays. After Wembury the River Yealm is crossed by ferry. It is then a pleasant walk through woods to join the old coach road round Gara Point to Warren Cottage and to Stoke Point, where there is a large caravan site below the path, and thence to Beacon Hill. The cliffs slope gently to the sea and at their foot are numerous small sandy coves. At Mothecombe House, home of the Mildmay family, the path goes inland to follow the road behind the house to Erme Mouth where it will be prudent to seek local advice about a point to ford the channel (and then only at low tide) since a ferry crossing may not be possible.

At Challaborough there are very extensive caravan sites but Bigbury is a pleasant place and on Burgh Island just offshore, which may be reached on foot across the sands only at low tide, there is a pleasant public house and a large hotel. It should be possible to cross the Avon by ferry but it will be necessary to attract attention across the river if coming from the west for the boat must come from Bantham; it would be dangerous to try to ford the river.

Between the Avon and Bolt Tail—where there is a good example of a promontory fort—a number of rivers in shallow marshy valleys come to the sea and provide easy road access to several sandy bays, as at Thurlestone Sands and Hope village. The easy access has made these bays extremely popular and there are many facilities for visitors. The cliffs with their browns, greens and yellows increase in grandeur, and reach 400ft as we approach Bolt Head on the way to Salcombe Harbour, the rock faces cut and twisted into weird forms and providing nesting places for sea-birds. Salcombe estuary is extremely attractive as are the inlets and creeks branching from the main channel, and they harbour much wildfowl. Salcombe, formerly a ship-building centre, is now a quiet and pleasant town in a splendid setting.

Prawle Point and Start Point

There is a passenger ferry to East Portlemouth and the path continues between cliff-top and field boundary to Prawle Point, the most southerly point in Devon where Lloyd's have a signal station and there is also a coastguard station. Like many of the headlands on the Devon and Cornish coasts, Prawle Point was the scene of many shipwrecks and on at least two occasions, in 1868 and 1873, tea clippers came to grief and the shore was piled high with tea. There are many coves below the cliff to Start Point, as on the west side of Salcombe Harbour, and wild flowers and sea-birds abound. At Start Point, where quartz veins may be seen in the rocks of the cliff face, there is a lighthouse and BBC radio masts. From the hard schist and serpentine rock of Start Point, which has resisted sea erosion, the coast sweeps backward and northward in a long graceful curve past Hallsands, Beesands and Torcross to the great shingle bank of Slapton Sands, second only to Chesil Beach in length, behind which has been formed the freshwater lake of Slapton Ley, now gradually silting up. There is fishing on the Ley, which is leased to the Council for Field Studies for scientific observation, and many species of birds may be seen here.

There is a road along the stone or shingle beach but easier walking may be found along the seaward verge to the point where the road takes a sharp bend up the hill westwards. This dangerous section of road is avoided by taking the old disused road straight northwards. The two roads join again, however, south of Strete, and then begins a section of the path where it proved too difficult to make a truly coastal path. The twisting narrow road follows the coastline and between it and the steeply shelving shoreline there are many large houses with private gardens. The path is designed primarily to avoid the busy road and follows minor lanes to the north and east of the road; in practice the road may be a convenient alternative.

The Dart to Seaton

The Dart estuary is of great beauty, and Dartmouth itself with its picturesque buildings steeped in maritime history and memories of Raleigh and of the explorers of the New World, will repay a few hours stay before taking the ferry to Kingswear. But the path from Kingswear to a mile south of Sharkham Point is not a right of way and until such time as one is made a route will have to be devised from the map making use of existing paths and lanes inland. At Berry Head there was, until quite recently, extensive quarrying at the headland, but this popular spot has now been made into a country park and provides good views. The harbour area of Brixham, once again a thriving fishing port, has much quaint and romantic interest as well as being a busy place.

The path leaves Brixham by the seafront ascending past the caravan site to Fishcombe Cove and along the edge of the golf course to Ebury Cove and Broad Sands and alongside the railway track to Paignton, which is followed by the large urban mass of Torquay, and after that by Teignmouth and Dawlish. There is much interesting coast from a point well within Torquay to the Teign estuary, but apart from that section the coast is much built up and is followed by the railway as far as Starcross. There are also many caravan sites and it will be convenient to resume the journey across the estuary of the Exe just east of Exmouth where Orcombe Point is the first headland followed by Straight Point. The quiet holiday town of Budleigh Salterton follows, where Sir John Millais painted 'The Boyhood of Raleigh', for Raleigh was born nearby. It is necessary to detour up the River Otter, to continue, still keeping strictly to the cliff edge, to Ladram Bay with its holiday caravans and the bustling holiday resort of Sidmouth. The geology has changed in this area and the cliffs are of red sandstone; at Torquay we left the Devonian rocks and entered the area of the New Red Sandstone and other more recent rocks.

The Landslip

The path ascends and descends the ridges of red soil which run transversely to the coast into Dunscombe and Branscombe to meet the first headland of white limestone at Beer Head (see below), where the coast and path turn abruptly through a caravan site into Beer and then Seaton. At Seaton the path veers slightly north round the golf course before entering the Landslip or Undercliff, from which it does not emerge until it reaches Lyme Regis, a distance of six miles. There is little opportunity in between for getting out of this rough and sometimes confusing area of woodland and scrub so it is best not to begin it late in the day. The most famous of the still-recurring landslips happened on Christmas Day 1839 when a great mass of land at Dowlands subsided—fields, crops, orchards, cottages and all—over the cliffs, and an island three-quarters of a mile long was at the same time temporarily uplifted from the sea. Water percolating through the pervious limestone forming the cliffs runs out where the limestone rests on impervious clay, and when the weight of the limestone reaches a certain point it simply

Beer Head, Devon (*Aerofilms Limited*)

fractures and slides over the clay. Minor landslips still occur from time to time and cracks in the earth will no doubt be seen. Over the years the sheltered and well watered landslipped area has become the habitat of the most varied collection of plants and birds and those interested in natural history will find this area a rich source of interest.

The *Dorset Coast Path* of 116km (72 miles) starts at Lyme Regis and sweeps eastwards along the long and gently curving Chesil Beach to the Portland peninsula and Weymouth. East of Weymouth, after Ringstead Bay, we approach one of the most attractive sections of the whole route, the chalk and limestone cliffs which include Lulworth Cove and Worbarrow Bay. Much of this area is of outstanding botanical and geological interest in addition to its natural beauty, and a long section has only recently been opened to public access after closure since the war. The cliff path continues along downland turf round St Aldhelm's Head to Swanage and Foreland Point to end at Studland on Poole Harbour. There is an alternative inland route across the chalk downs of the Purbeck Hills overlooking Weymouth.

Lyme Regis and Golden Cap

Lyme Regis, where the coast path begins, is best known for the Cobb, its associations with Jane Austen (it is said to be the setting for *Sense and Sensibility*) and for the landing of the Duke of Monmouth in 1685. After the defeat of the Pretender at the Battle of Sedgemoor twelve local men were condemned by Judge Jeffreys and hanged on the Cobb where Monmouth had landed.

Between Lyme Regis and Charmouth is a further landslipped black clay area of tumbled earth and scrub at the Spittles and Black Ven. The path avoids this area of broken ground and dense vegetation and skirts the golf course well back from the sea; even this line has had to be re-adjusted to take account of more recent local landslips. It is not uncommon to find fossils in the stratified rocks of this area and it was the ichthyosaurus found on the beach at Black Ven in 1811 by ten-year-old Mary Anning that gave rise to the science of palaeontology. Beyond Charmouth there are still more areas of old landslips and the path keeps well back from the cliffs before returning to ascend Golden Cap, whose crown of glowing yellow sandstone dominates this length of coast; and then down to the few houses of Seatown where there is road access and refreshments in summer. Three miles of cliff-top walking brings us to the harbour of West Bay, a small port and sailing resort.

Chesil Beach

At West Bay begins the shingle bank which becomes Chesil Beach. Starting as fine shingle, the stones become imperceptibly larger until, at the Isle of Portland, eighteen miles away, they are sizeable boulders. The stones are first swept to Portland by tides and currents from the Devon and Dorset coasts to the west and are rounded, polished and reduced in size by attrition as they are pushed back along West Bay. The volume of stones, mostly limestone and quartz, is enormous and the average height of the shingle beach is some sixty feet and the width some 200yds. The slingstones unearthed at the Iron Age fort of Maiden Castle near Dorchester are identical with those to be found on Chesil Beach. Roman coins have been found on the beach and many ships have been

wrecked on it, or even washed over it during exceptional storms.
The path continues along Burton Cliffs, and on the landward side of the beach past Burton Mere to the start of the Fleet at Abbotsbury. The Fleet is a long strip of water locked in by the shingle beach and stretching the whole way to Weymouth, being able to escape only through the narrow neck of water which separates the Isle of Portland from the mainland. Chesil Beach, though impressive to look at, is tedious to walk on after a time, so the coast path turns slightly inland round Chapel Hill close to the famous swannery on the edge of the Fleet, which dates back at least to the fourteenth century. At Abbotsbury there is a medieval tithe-barn to be seen, together with the remains of St Peter's Abbey and the fifteenth-century St Catherine's Chapel perched on Chapel Hill, as well as thatched cottages on the raised pavement of the main street.

The Dorset section, below the cliffs, west of Eype's Mouth, looking east

Abbotsbury

Before Abbotsbury is reached, at West Bexington, the inland alternative route begins, taking a course along the high land of the Purbeck Hills. The lower path from Abbotsbury continues its general direction to join the shore of the Fleet at Langton Herring, and follows its winds and twists to Weymouth. Views from this low shoreline are limited and although it has a quiet charm many people who are not seeking accommodation in Weymouth will prefer to take the hill route, which offers a change from sea views (although the sea is distantly visible for most of the way).

Hardy Monument

View from White Horse Hill on the inland section of the south-west path looking towards the sea

The two routes join again at Osmington Mills, west of Portland Bill.

Hardy Country

The inland route from West Bexington turns quickly from the shore up through the village to the road, later crossing it and going round the north of Abbotsbury Castle, a hill-fort, to the Hardy Monument by way of the turf tracks of Wears Hill and White Hill. From the high ground of the ridges formed by these hills there are good views across the farmed land that drops away towards the coast path and Chesil Beach. The path crosses the Abbotsbury road and continues along hedgerows to the top of Portesham Hill, where it continues inside and on the seaward side of roads. From the 800ft-high site of the Hardy Monument (see left)— the Hardy in question is Nelson's Hardy, not the novelist—which is visible from almost everywhere in Dorset, there are exceptionally fine views. A broad track, still following the high ground, leads due east over Bronkham Hills to the Dorchester–Weymouth road about one mile south of Maiden Castle, which should be visited if possible. The massive Iron Age and British fortress was stormed by the Romans under Vespasian in AD43 and abandoned thereafter. Skeletons of those who died in the encounter have been uncovered outside the ramparts, which comprise three concentric earthen embankments up to 60ft high and two miles in circumference. Up to 5,000 people are thought to have lived there in wooden huts in its heyday. The burial places of notables among these and earlier peoples will be seen scattered throughout the area in the form of tumuli, some of them close to the path, indicating the importance of the district in Iron Age and earlier times. The foundations of a temple built during the Roman occupation are visible within the site.

The path continues eastwards by Bincombe Down to the hamlet of

Bincombe and skirts the circular earthworks of Chalbury Hill-fort before taking to the ridge of West and East Hills and White Horse Hill, where the famous white horse and rider were cut in 1808 to commemorate the visit of King George III in 1789, when it is said he came to try one of the first bathing machines ever to be used. These chalk hills and those already traversed by the inland route are reminiscent of the North and South Downs with short, springy turf, smoothly rounded hills, and their great wealth of prehistoric sites. The inland route continues through Osmington village to meet the sea and rejoin the coastal route.

Weymouth

The coastal route re-starts east of Weymouth at Overcombe and goes on to Bowleaze Cove, past the holiday camp, past Redcliffe Point and the landslip area of Black Head, to Osmington Mills, where the two routes link up, and then on to Ringstead Bay. Here oil has been extracted from the shale in commercial quantities for many years. After White Nothe at the east end of the bay the path approaches one of the most scenically rewarding long stretches of the Dorset Path, characterised by short grass, gentle slopes and a pleasing harmony of colours, past Swyre Head, Durdle Door and Dungy Head to Lulworth Cove. Here the path originally stopped, blocked by the Tyneham tank ranges which for thirty years after the war denied access to eight miles of some of the most attractive scenery and some of the most interesting areas for ecology and geology on the whole peninsula route, and requiring a wide detour of twenty miles to regain the coast again at Kimmeridge. In January 1975 it was announced in Parliament that the coast path would be re-opened at certain times once it had been made safe from unexploded shells. The coast is now available for 46 weekends each year, for 16 days at Christmas, 7 days at Easter, 7 days during the Spring Bank Holiday and 7 weeks in the summer. Wardens guide the public and ensure their safety.

Lulworth to Swanage

The coast now opened up includes the eastern side of Lulworth Cove and the long Worbarrow and Brandy Bays and the greater part of Kimmeridge Bay, areas about which it might be said in retrospect that they have derived some benefit from their long military occupation, since they have been protected from all forms of post-war 'development'. On this coast the band of limestone which formed the original cliffs has been breached by the sea to reveal at the back of the bays the parallel band of chalk which runs behind the limestone, so that the 'horns' of the bays, as at Mupe Rocks and Worbarrow Tout, are of limestone while the inner cliffs are of chalk. At Kimmeridge, however, the cliffs are of clay and shale with wide black ledges stretching out to sea at their feet, and the dark colouring is less attractive. Within reach of the path is Smedmore House, which is open to the public.

The rocks at Chapman's Pool, a small circular bay reached after a stiff climb over Houndstout Cliff, are also dark, but ahead looms the high and massive limestone promontory of St Aldhelm's Head, which is reached by a path coming below the cliff-top. There is a Norman chapel, and immense views, at the top of the Head, and craggy rocks at its foot. Round the headland the path continues in a curve past Dancing Ledge (so called because of the play of the waves on the reefs) to Durlston Head,

Fulmar

where there is now a country park. The Tilly Whim Caves are cut deep into the rocks and are in fact disused quarries from which Purbeck Stone has been extracted. Durlston Castle is modern and is now a municipal refreshment house and entertainments centre, and nearby is the Great Globe of the world in Portland Stone. The path continues through woodland and then by crumbling limestone cliffs to Peveril Point, whence a savage reef juts out, as much a peril to today's leisure sailors in Swanage Bay as it was to the Danes whose fleet was wrecked on it in AD877. A monument to the event, curiously topped by a cannon ball, stands on the front in Swanage.

North of Swanage the path proceeds along the sea edge on the way to Ballard Down and out to Ballard Point and thence along the broad swathe of turf above the chalk cliffs to the Foreland where the sea-girt limestone figures of Old Harry and his wife offshore are being rapidly reduced in stature by erosion. From the Downs one can look across Poole Harbour or across to the cliffs of the Isle of Wight where, after crossing the sea-bed, the chalk re-appears. A sharp change of direction brings the path to Studland village and beyond it stretches the heathland of Studland National Nature Reserve. From the north end of Shell Bay the Sandbank ferry will bring the walker to Poole and Bournemouth.

6 · The Offa's Dyke Path

Opened: 10 July 1971
Length: 168 miles (271km)

Offa's Dyke Information Centre (run by Offa's Dyke Association)
Knighton—The Old School

Offa's Dyke

The Offa's Dyke path of 217km (168 miles) follows the course of an earthwork which dates from the Dark Ages and is probably the most remarkable surviving monument of that period in Britain. (For scenic reasons, and to take advantage of fine walking country, the path departs substantially from the line of Offa's Dyke at two places where little trace remains of the dyke, to cross the Black Mountains and to follow the escarpment overlooking the Vale of Clwyd.)

The principles governing the alignment of Offa's Dyke are not entirely clear and even its purpose is not beyond dispute, but it would appear that when the westward drive of the Saxon invaders had spent itself against the mountainous area which now forms the eastern boundary of Wales, the Saxon King Offa undertook the task, well before AD800, of establishing the western boundary of his kingdom of Mercia with the warlike Britons who had retreated before his people into their mountain fastnesses beyond. The belief that Offa's Dyke was not a defensive work like Hadrian's Wall is supported by an examination of the chosen terrain. It does not run from peak to peak and often prefers the lower ground. Sometimes it is strongest where natural features appear to provide a more attractive defensive position, as along the limestone cliffs above the River Wye, but is absent where there is no natural barrier, as across the Hereford plain. Attempts have been made to explain the gaps by supposing that dense forests, now long cleared, existed in such places and provided a sufficient barrier. Sometimes Offa's Dyke runs east–west instead of north–south, or is duplicated, as if the plans had been changed in the course of construction. A solution of these problems is not helped by the existence of another, shorter earthwork, Wat's Dyke, apparently serving the same purpose some distance to the east from Oswestry northwards; this was probably an earlier prototype of Offa's Dyke constructed when the fortunes of war were less favourable to the Saxons.

A general principle that may be observed is that Offa's Dyke is usually on ground from which the land occupied by the Welsh could be

Offa's Dyke signpost

overlooked, and the ditch formed by taking the earth to build the dyke is generally on the western side. The not infrequent departures from this principle have suggested that the work, though clearly executed in accordance with a master plan, was delegated to local overlords who carried it out without close supervision and were perhaps not themselves entrusted with too much information on what it was all about.

Although much reduced in size by the effects of time and agricultural use the line can be traced from Sedbury Cliffs on the Severn estuary near Chepstow to Prestatyn in North Wales, a distance, so far as the Offa's Dyke Path is concerned, of 168 miles. Just under 70 miles of the path are along Offa's Dyke. An authoritative study of and commentary on the dyke made by Sir Cyril Fox before the war and published as *Offa's Dyke* provides much information about the origin and construction of the earthwork. It is likely that it reached a height of 20ft with a ditch 10ft wide, and it may have been topped with stakes and have had openings with gates and crossing points. It is suggested that the vagaries of the line may be explained if it is accepted that it was erected by mutual consent between King Offa and the Welsh princes with a certain amount of give and take about where it should run. Apart from simply marking the boundary of Offa's dominion the dyke may have acted as a kind of customs line and may have enabled punishment to be meted out to members of the rival peoples found on the wrong side in the course of cattle raids or other forays. In any case the dyke came to be regarded in the course of time as the natural border between the cultures and languages of the two peoples and the modern boundary between England and Wales is very largely along it. For its time, and bearing in mind the implements, skills and social organisation available, the building of the dyke was a considerable achievement. Today the walker on the long distance path will see it in places as only a slight hump in a field; sometimes it is built into hedgebanks which are indistinguishable from any other hedgebank, or is buried among trees; but in other places, particularly in Shropshire and the north central areas, it will be seen loping for miles across open countryside, unmistakable for what it is.

Border Country

Although the dyke provides a continuous historic theme for the whole route, the immediate area of the path and the Welsh border in general is of much wider historical interest. The low hills between the Welsh mountains to the west and the English plains to the east form a transition zone where peoples have mingled for centuries and have often come into conflict. The Romans were content to make their presence felt in this area, but otherwise interfered little with the communities of Celtic tribes under their local chieftains. Forts and a connecting road were built (such a fort is Caer Fforda on the route in the Severn valley) from which punitive raids could be made against the warlike tribes in retaliation for plundering attacks on the lowlands. These people lived in encampments of which examples may be seen along the path in the Clwydian Hills; they no doubt carried out sacrifices in woodland glades, as described by Tacitus. They were strong enough to rise in revolt in the first century AD under Caractacus, whose name is preserved in placenames along the border.

When the Romans left, the attacks from the Angles and Saxons began, and when they reached the coast at the Bristol Channel and the River Dee they isolated the West Britons from their compatriots in the rest of the island, along the line which was later to be formalised by the construction of Offa's Dyke. The Welsh border was then a battle zone where the Britons, though weaker in arms and organisation in the open, could retreat to the safety of the hills where they remained supreme. Under pressure the Welsh tribes gradually formed themselves into larger groupings and became powerful enough to act alone or ally themselves with their Mercian neighbours in campaigns against the rival Saxon kingdoms of Northumbria and Wessex. Their power grew so that immediately before the Norman Conquest they were able to secure some remarkable successes, particularly under Gruffydd ap Llewellyn, in various shifting combinations with Saxons, Danes and Vikings, or even independently in the plains, including victories at Welshpool in 1039, at Leominster in 1052 and Hereford in 1058. Few physical reminders of this period remain except in placenames and romantic associations with the legendary King Arthur, whose origin is in this period, as at Knucklas Castle near the route north-west of Knighton.

Chepstow Castle

The Normans quickly advanced westwards and established great earldoms for the protection of the Marches at Hereford, Shrewsbury and Chester, with less powerful but much more numerous marcher lordships along the actual frontier. With their superior organisation, arms and skills they soon established their authority against Welsh and Saxon alike and founded castles along the route at Chepstow (see above), White Castle, Clun, Chirk, Powis and in many other places. Chirk and Powis, in altered form, remain inhabited to this day. Remote from the English kings they exercised near-absolute power over their serfs of mixed national origin, quarrelling among themselves but ever watchful for attacks from the Welsh mountains. They were never entirely secure however against attacks from the Welsh princes and there were frequent revolts, culminating in that of Owain Glyndwr in the opening years of the fifteenth century.

Settled agricultural practices were introduced under the Norman system of land tenure and towns grew up as centres for the surrounding area. The old Celtic and Saxon churches were dismantled and grand new churches and religious houses, particularly of the Cistercian order, were built on the sites. These castles, churches, abbeys and towns are features of interest along the route. None of the towns have grown to any great extent. Their stirring history of warfare and bloodshed long behind them, they now have an old-world character of a quiet, sleepy charm. Their greatest activity today is likely to be on market days, and the walker will be lucky if he happens to pass through or visit them for accommodation on these days.

Scenery

It is, however, the scenic quality of the border area that must be the route's primary justification. Extensive areas of open heathland are included—the Black Mountains, the Berwyns and the Clwydian range—but the central stretches, as in the Radnor and Clun Forests, are across areas of small, rounded, steep-sided hills broken up in small fields, where one hill follows the other with hills of similar height in the view all around. Many pleasant valleys of east-flowing rivers are crossed where they run to join the Wye, the Severn or the Dee. We cross the fields of

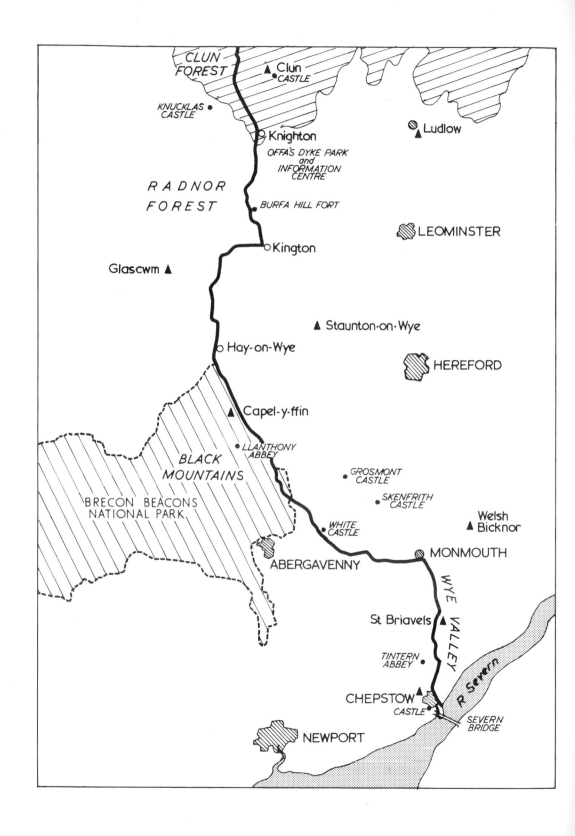

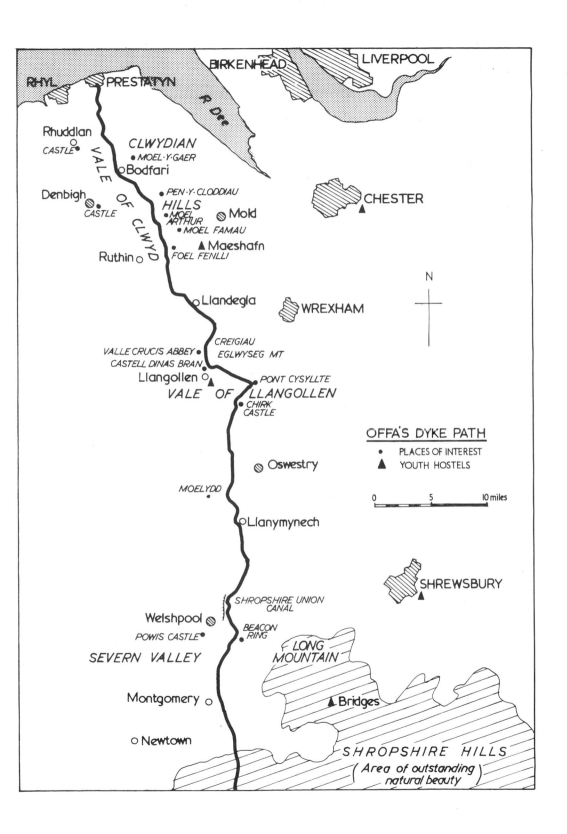

RHYL
BIRKENHEAD
LIVERPOOL
PRESTATYN
R. Dee

Rhuddlan
CASTLE
CLWYDIAN
• MOEL·Y·GAER
Bodfari

Denbigh
CASTLE
• PEN·Y·CLODDIAU
HILLS
MOEL
ARTHUR
◎ Mold
• MOEL FAMAU
CHESTER
▲

Ruthin ○
VALE OF CLWYD
▲ Maeshafn
FOEL FENLLI

○ Llandegla
◎ WREXHAM
N

VALLE CRUCIS ABBEY •
CREIGIAU
EGLWYSEG MT
CASTELL DINAS BRAN •
Llangollen ○ ▲
PONT CYSYLLTE
VALE OF LLANGOLLEN
• CHIRK
CASTLE

OFFA'S DYKE PATH
• PLACES OF INTEREST
▲ YOUTH HOSTELS

◎ Oswestry

MOELYDD •

0   5   10 miles

○ Llanymynech

SHREWSBURY
▲

SHROPSHIRE UNION
CANAL
Welshpool ◎
POWIS CASTLE •
BEACON
RING
LONG
MOUNTAIN
SEVERN VALLEY

Montgomery ○
▲ Bridges

○ Newtown
SHROPSHIRE HILLS
(Area of outstanding
natural beauty)

the broken but flattish plain of Hereford and follow part of the meandering course of the Severn, or look down from above on the Wye. The views are mainly into the heart of Wales, as one would expect, extending in the far north as far as Snowdonia. It is a country of sparse population, seemingly forgotten by the modern world, a land of isolated sheep and pasture farms, of tumbling streams and ruined castles, of small fields with many hedgerow trees and spinneys but also with many new plantations. In these areas the route passes along lanes, crosses many stiles, goes through woods, joins and leaves minor roads and there are so many twists and turns that route finding can be a problem.

The route was opened by Lord Hunt in July 1971 at Knighton at a ceremony in which the Offa's Dyke Association played a leading part. This voluntary society, which is dedicated to fostering the use and development of the long distance path, gave valuable help to the Countryside Commission in the later stages of the completion of the route and in ensuring that the paths were cleared and signposted. Membership is open to users and intending users of the path and strip maps and an accommodation list are available. The secretary of the association may be contacted at the address given in the Appendix.

The Route: Chepstow and the Wye

The *Offa's Dyke Path* begins at Sedbury cliffs on the Severn estuary, a mile or so east of Chepstow. To start at the very beginning you have to take the Beachley road as far as Buttington Tump, turn south-east into a field, and follow the line of the dyke as far as the cliff edge where there is a fine view of the Severn and the Severn Bridge. Return to the road at The Tump, and follow the line of the dyke through new housing estates to the banks of the Wye. Many people will, however, choose to start at Chepstow and take the opportunity to see the old town with its steep streets, fragments of the thirteenth-century town walls (the Port Walk) and the town gate, and in particular its Norman castle perched on limestone cliffs 70ft above the River Wye. The castle was begun by William Fitz Osborn, a companion of William the Conqueror, and is thus one of the earliest of the Norman strongholds in Wales. It was extended in the twelfth and thirteenth centuries and fell into disrepair in Stuart times, not having withstood an attack until the time of the Civil War.

From Chepstow, after crossing the road bridge, the route begins at a turning off the St Briavels road near Tutshill. The Wye, the east bank of which is followed for fifteen miles into Monmouth, winds its way in great loops through its famous gorge, its banks thickly clad with mature woodland of oak and beech. Since this is limestone country, the area is colourful with wild flowers. The path takes a course between the St Briavels road and the river to the great declivity at Wintour's Leap, the legendary site where a horseman made a prodigious leap down to the river to escape his pursuers during the Civil War; here the river suddenly appears spread out far below. A mile further on at Dennel Hill the path finally disentangles itself from the St Briavels road by turning left to pick up the dyke in thick woodland, but the earthwork only achieves remarkable proportions at Shorn Cliff where the bank and ditch have been encroached upon by the surrounding trees. For size and impressiveness this is one of the best sections of the dyke along the whole route, and in openings through the trees there are fine views across to the

romantic ruins of Tintern Abbey (see above), the best being from the
Devil's Pulpit. This Cistercian foundation dates from 1131 and its setting
has inspired many painters, as well as Wordsworth. The construction of
the dyke at such an expenditure of effort along the river as far as
Monmouth, where the river itself would appear to be a sufficient
demarcation, underlines the significance of the dyke as a symbolic and
permanent frontier line, a warning that anyone crossing it did so at his
own risk; it would appear to have had little military significance.

Tintern Abbey from Offa's Dyke
path above the Wye

The path emerges from the woods and crosses St Briavels Common
along lanes and across fields, from where fragments of the dyke may be
seen, to Bigsweir; from here to Redbrook, still along the top of the
wooded gorge, the route follows further fragments of the dyke. It is now
two miles into Monmouth along an open ridge above the river, passing at
the top of Kymin Hill a monument erected to the memory of Nelson's
admirals; the 800ft hill makes a fine viewpoint. Monmouth, where the
Wye and Monnow meet, was an important point of entry into Wales in
Roman as well as Norman times. The castle no longer exists, apart from
the twelfth-century Great Tower, but the thirteenth-century gatehouse on
the old Monnow Bridge (which the walker will cross) is unique of its
kind (see right). Geoffrey of Monmouth, twelfth-century churchman,
historian, and chronicler of the tales of King Arthur, was a prior in the
town, and Henry V was a native; Nelson was also a frequent visitor with
Lady Hamilton, and there is a statue in Agincourt Square to Rolls of Rolls-
Royce, who was also born there.

Monnow Bridge gatehouse

The Monmouth Plain

Between Monmouth and the southern foothills of the Black Mountains the path runs first westwards and then north-westwards with many twists and turns, for seventeen miles, through an area of small foothills, an agricultural landscape of fields, woods and streams and occasionally a small hamlet. From the built-up outskirts of Monmouth the route takes us west up through King's Wood and down to the Trothy Valley, leaving it for Llanvihangel and on to Llantilio Crossenny, where the moat of the vanished manor house of Hen Gwrt is of interest. In just over two miles we come to the White Castle, one of three in the area (the other two being at Skenfrith and Grosmont), evidence of the importance attached to the northern approaches to Monmouth in Norman times. White Castle, which belonged to the de Burgh lordship, is on a hilltop and is surrounded by a water-filled moat which includes a small island (actually a defensive work); there are good views of the Skirrid to the west.

The Black Mountains

After crossing the Trothy south of Caggle Street the path follows the course of the stream to Llangattock Lingoed and thence down again to the valley of the Monnow in its upper reaches and the Abergavenny road. We are now about to begin the ascent of the long, bare easternmost ridge of the Black Mountains on the eastern boundary of the Brecon Beacons National Park where it towers above the Olchon valley on the one hand and the Llanthony valley on the other, the highest point rising to over 2,300ft. The fifteen-mile section across the Black Mountains is a hard day's walk in good weather over grass moorland, interspersed with heather, bilberry and crowberry, and in bad weather or in mist it may be as well to have second thoughts about tackling it. Having crossed the road and river the path climbs up by Tre-fedw and Bwlch farms to the Iron Age camp at Pen-twyn and on to Hatterrall Hill. Steep slopes, bare or thorn-covered at the tops, plunge down on either side as we proceed along the ridge, the red sandstone slopes scoured by numerous short, sharp streams. Down in the Llanthony valley beside the Afon Honddu are the remains of the twelfth-century Augustinian priory of St Anthony, founded by Hugh de Lacy, Marcher Lord of Hereford, on the site of an earlier chapel dedicated to St David. Further up the valley, at Capel-y-ffin, are the remains of the more recent St Anthony Abbey, a Benedictine foundation of 1870 which was abandoned some forty years later. The sites of both were chosen for their peacefulness and seclusion, and it would seem that the natural beauty of the place has not changed much since the twelfth century, for the much-travelled Giraldus has left a glowing account of it made during a visit to the priory in about 1180. There is also a youth hostel at Capel-y-ffin, but not much other accommodation, not even in the scattered farmsteads, many of which are now in ruins.

The busy market town of Hay is built on high ground above the Wye where the river valley is broad and open. Like many other border towns it has the remains of a castle, which was burned down by Owain Glyndwr, and alongside is a seventeenth-century manor house. It makes a good centre for visiting the numerous other border castles as well as the churches, and Roman, Norman and medieval sites of interest in the area. The flat valley bottom from Hay is crossed to Bronydd and the path climbs steeply to the head of Bettws Dingle and thence by lanes and field

paths to the hilltop crowned by Pen-twyn prehistoric camp and down to
Newchurch in the Arrow valley. A path across the grassy top of
Disgwylfa Hill leads us down to Gladestry village, from which we ascend
to the long ridge and steep north-facing slopes of Hergest Ridge, with
views west to Radnor Forest and eastwards over Hereford, following the
ridge straight down into Kington. Before entering the town the path
passes the moated manor of Hergest Croft, the gardens and parkland of
which may be visited. Hergest gave its name to *The White Book of Hergest*
and *The Red Book of Hergest*, legendary Welsh tales which were written
down in the area. These hills are typical of the thinly populated Radnor
countryside through which the route passes, with hill succeeding hill all
around, steep grassy slopes to climb, and a patchwork of green fields and
woodland in every view, a beautiful area which the twentieth century
seems to have forgotten. The dyke, however, which re-appears strongly
further on, is not evident in this area, possibly because in Offa's time the
woodland was dense enough to make it unnecessary.

Leaving Kington we climb steeply up towards Bradnor Hill but pass
round its eastern flanks to meet the dyke again at Rushock Hill where,
having come from the English direction, it changes course to run due
north from hilltop to hilltop more or less continuously the whole ten miles
to Knighton. We come down to cross the footbridge over Hindwell
Brook, and climb up again beneath the ramparts of Burfa Iron Age Camp
and up again to Evenjobb Hill; then on to Pen Offa farm where there is a
good section of Offa's Dyke and Castlering Camp on the hill below, and
then down to the River Lugg past Yew Tree Farm, where there is also a

The Dyke at Beggar's Bush, near
Presteign, Radnor Forest

good section of dyke. The Radnorshire farms on or close to the dyke are themselves often of great age and architectural interest, and as more accommodation is being offered because of the use being made of the long distance path, local inquiries could be made with advantage. Some distance up-stream in the Lugg valley at Pilleth is the site of a great Welsh victory over the Earl of Mortimer in 1402 at the height of Owain Glyndwr's rebellion. The earl was captured, changed sides and married Glyndwr's daughter. From the Lugg valley the path and the dyke rise to Furrow Hill and follow a ridge which eventually drops down into Knighton.

Knighton

Knighton, or Tref-y-clawdd (the town of the dyke) lies on the River Teme surrounded by wooded hills. In the town, off the road to the west, is the Offa's Dyke Park, opened by the Offa's Dyke Association on the occasion of the inauguration of the Offa's Dyke Path on the site in July 1971. A section of the dyke is in the park, and also a stone monument erected to commemorate the opening of the path. The old primary school nearby has been repaired and re-opened as a youth hostel, with rooms in which an information centre about the dyke and path and the surrounding area is run by the Mid-Wales Tourist Council; some rooms have also been taken over by the Offa's Dyke Association.

From Knighton the path, having followed the River Teme for a short section and crossed it by the wooden footbridge alongside the railway, crosses the railway and road to climb up along the edge of the forest to Panpunton Hill. It continues to Sanaham Hill with views across the Teme

The view at Clunbury, Shropshire (*Crown Copyright*)

valley where the site of Knucklas Castle can be picked out. First an Iron Age fort, the isolated hill at the confluence of the Teme and the Ffrwdwen Brook became a stronghold of the Mortimers to whom the town of Knighton was granted by Henry III; but legend says that it was the abode of a giant whose daughter Guinevere was married to King Arthur. From Cwm Sanaham Hill the Offa's Dyke Path continues to Llanfair Hill where the road running parallel to the dyke must be used, but the dyke can be clearly seen in the fields a short distance away. The dyke is rejoined at Springhill Farm and runs sharply down to the River Clun.

In this section and in the succeeding one as far as Montgomery the dyke is at its best, running for miles up hill and down dale and along valley sides as a clear feature in the Shropshire landscape.

At Mellington Hall we drop down from the forest of Clun to the Montgomery plain, the valley of the Severn and the kingdom of Powis. Here the dyke, still well marked, runs straight over the flat land to Lymore Park, now a caravan site. Montgomery town, a mile to the west of the path, is now a quiet place, but has interesting Regency and Georgian buildings. It had a town wall, the ditch of which is still traceable, and a castle first built by Roger de Montgomery in 1072. The castle was destroyed in the border wars, rebuilt in 1221 and lasted until the Civil Wars of the seventeenth century; now only fragments remain.

The Long Mountain and the Severn

North of Montgomery the path crosses the Camlad River by the road bridge, but instead of continuing down to the Severn, as one might expect, the dyke then turns and runs parallel to the river past the village of Forden and along the foothills of the Long Mountain. The path, however, takes neither of these two courses, but deliberately ascends to Beacon Ring on the top of the Long Mountain for the magnificent views over the winding valley of the river and towards the Shropshire hills in the other direction. Halfway up the slope the path goes through woodland where magnificent stands of *Sequoia* may be seen. From the hill-fort at Beacon Ring one also looks directly across the Severn to Powis Castle and Park and the town of Welshpool. The powerful princes of Powis kept themselves somewhat apart during the centuries of border warfare, sometimes siding with their Welsh compatriots, sometimes with the Normans, and so managing to survive as an Earldom of Powis, at least in name, for the succession has long since died out. The sandstone castle, called Castell Goch (red castle), was built in the fourteenth century but has been much modernised. It has a deer park and gardens laid out by Capability Brown, and in the park woodland is a fir tree which, at over 160ft, is said to be the tallest in Britain. Welshpool has some Georgian buildings; a narrow gauge railway up the Nant-y-Caws Brook has recently been re-opened.

The path descends steeply from the Long Mountain by Hope village and crosses the Severn at Buttington road bridge. Crossings of the river were important even before the days of border warfare, and the original ford was the scene of battles between Saxons and Danes, and Saxons and Welsh. The path follows the bank of the river but leaves it for a short distance to follow the busy A483 road and then the towpath of the Shropshire Union Canal as far as Pool Quay. It is worth noting here how a course has been cut for the canal along the contours of the steep hillside

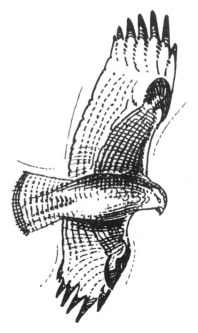

Buzzard

above the road so that the watercourse appears suspended above the valley. Reverting to the river again the route follows the flood banks for three miles before leaving the Severn and cutting across to Llandysilio and the road bridge across the Severn near Llanymynech.

To Chirk Castle and the Dee

Beyond Llanymynech, half in Wales and half in England, the path climbs Llanymynech Hill, once mined for copper and now for limestone. We follow the line of the dyke round the western slopes of this hill but where the dyke continues over the following hill we leave it because of the much more extensive limestone workings at Porth-y-Waen, and take a roundabout and intricate course to the west along roads, lanes and footpaths to avoid the scarred area. But in so doing we ascend to the top of the Moelydd, a hill where the extensive views are more than adequate compensation.

We rejoin the dyke at Trefonen and follow it to the 'edge' at Craig Forda, where we can look from our vantage point deep into the Welsh hills over the trees that cascade steeply at our feet. Although the dyke runs along this edge it turns to plunge into the woods, but we keep our height along the old racecourse as far as the Oswestry road. Baker's Hill lies just across the road and there is a good section of dyke, and good views, on its western side, but it has been necessary to forego a path here, and the route must follow the road to Carreg-y-big Farm.

From Carreg-y-big the dyke is followed northward past Orseddwen and Selattyn Hill to Craignant, and eventually down to the narrow Ceiriog valley with Chirk Castle grounds on its far side. The castle, built in 1310 by the Mortimers, has been inhabited by the Myddleton family since 1595, and in spite of sieges and damage during the Civil War is substantially unaltered. The dyke itself runs through the park (and through the park lake) and may be seen when the grounds are open; at other times it is necessary to detour westwards round the park perimeter.

The River Dee is crossed by road some three miles downstream from

The dyke near Oswestry

Llangollen, but some walkers will prefer to take the canal towpath and cross by Telford's Pontcysyllte aqueduct (built in 1805) where there is a path alongside the canal which is carried over the river at a height of 120ft. At Trevor Hall the path joins the Precipice Walk, a surfaced track curving round below the barren limestone crags of the Eglwyseg Rocks, which overlook the Vale of Llangollen and give distant views across to the mountains of Snowdonia. There is much of interest in the area apart from Llangollen itself. Between the path and Llangollen is a conical hill surmounted by the remains of a medieval castle of the princes of Powis, and earlier earthworks, Castell Dynas Bran. Valle Crucis Abbey, founded in 1189, is also overlooked by the path further on; and the famous Horseshoe Pass is in the same area. From the little cwm at World's End at the far end of the Eglwyseg Rocks the path strikes out and up over open country by a track which leads eventually down to Llandegla.

The Clwydian Range

From Llandegla northwards the route begins its last distinctive long section along the escarpment of the rounded Clwydian Hills, of Silurian sandstone, which overlook the fertile Vale of Clwyd to the west, with the historic towns of Ruthin, Denbigh, St Asaph and Rhuddlan strung along it, each with its castle (except St Asaph, which has a cathedral instead). Further away the view stretches across the hills of Denbigh to Snowdonia. Offa's Dyke is now lost somewhere to the east. The path skirts, or climbs to the summit of, a succession of bracken- and grass-covered hills, the bare slopes of which, however, are becoming increasingly covered by conifer plantations. A number of these hilltops—Moel Fenlli, Moel Arthur, Pen-y-Cloddiau and Moel y Gaer—are crowned by massive earthworks, which are particularly impressive because of the space they enclose. From Bodfari onwards the country is less bare and open but is nonetheless extremely attractive and undulating and the path makes more use of lanes and country roads down to Rhuallt and beyond, finally dropping down to the sea at Prestatyn.

7 · The Cleveland Way

Opened: 24 May 1969

Length 93 miles (150km)

	Ordnance Survey Map Reference:

National Park Information Centres:

Helmsley The Old Vicarage, Bondgate (Tel 657/8)   SE 613 838

Sutton Bank (Tel 657/8)   SE 515 829

Thirsk (Tel 426)   SE 515 831

A Moors and Coast Path

The Cleveland Way is 150km (93 miles) long, and makes a great loop round the high rim of the Yorkshire Moors National Park from Helmsley to near Filey. It consists of two distinct sections. An inland section takes in magnificent moorland scenery overlooking the Vale of York along the lonely Hambleton and Cleveland Hills and curves round the valley of the lower Tees south of Middlesbrough, to meet the sea at Saltburn. From here a coast path keeps to the edge of some of the highest and most spectacular cliffs along the whole east coast, passing through small fishing and holiday villages and the towns of Whitby and Scarborough and giving over most of its length good views of coast and moorland.

Many miles of clearly defined and easy paths and green roads are included in the moorland route, particularly over the gentler slopes of the Hambleton Hills, but parts of the Cleveland Hills are fairly demanding, with some steep climbs and long treks over open heather moor, which can be tiring. After heavy rain boggy patches can develop, due to poor drainage. Since the path keeps to the moor edge, however, with the moors on one side and the Vale of York far below on the other, route-finding is not a serious problem, though there will always be local difficulties even in good weather when close attention to the map is necessary in order to avoid the frustration of taking the wrong route and ending up far from where one should be. Sometimes a light mist (known locally as 'roak') drifts in from the sea on summer days when the air over the land becomes heated and rises. The reduced visibility calls for greater care, particularly in those places where the path is on slippery boulder clay, as is often the case along the coast. The cliffs are also high and sheer and are subject to erosion, so a close watch is needed, especially where, as often happens, the path runs between field boundary fences and a sheer drop. The path is signposted 'Moors Path' and 'Coast Path' respectively.

Geology: Jet, Alum and Iron

The upland area through which the path runs has had a long and varied history, both in the geological and human timescales. The solid rocks were laid down in Jurassic times and are composed of sandstones, limestones and shales, the earlier liassic rocks being most important for the economic life of the surrounding area. These rocks produced the alum, jet and ironstone which have been won from the earliest times and gave rise to the great industrial complex of Middlesbrough in the nineteenth century. Middlesbrough had a population of 150 in 1830 and 7,000 in 1850, this and subsequent much greater rises in population being due to the mineral wealth discovered along the Cleveland Hills and the coast. The evidence of these workings remains along the escarpment and along practically the whole of the sea cliffs, where the beds were exposed, but time, the encroachment of plant and tree growth, and to some extent the nature of the workings have ensured that the scars are not obtrusive and they remain largely as features of interest rather than serious blots on the landscape.

After the Jurassic beds had been uplifted from the sea they formed a great dome, which was subsequently folded and shaped by the forces of erosion. The coast and the area surrounding the moors, but not the central moors themselves, were then covered by ice. When the glaciers receded they had planed off the surface areas beneath the ice, exposing the underlying rocks and incidentally filling in any depressions, particularly on the coast, with the boulder clay and gravels that they carried before them. Small streams have cut deep courses in this softer material over the cliffs and escarpments. While the rocks of the moors are therefore mainly of the original sandstone, the underlying limestones and shales are exposed along their edges, as they are to some extent also in the dales which cut into the moorland mass. Along the slopes of the Cleveland (ie cliff-land) Hills small heaps of spoil indicate points where jet was extracted from adits driven into the hillsides. Jet, a form of fossilised wood, was much admired in ancient and medieval times, when it could be picked up on the shore, and was used for ornaments, beads and crosses, but suffered a decline until the fashion for jet ornaments revived in Victorian times, when outcrops were exploited along the escarpment, the coast and in the dales. The industry, once a lucrative trade in Whitby, is now almost defunct.

Alum is used in tanning and dyeing and was manufactured from shales which were burned and then leached, the resulting liquid being concentrated by boiling and allowed to crystallise. Suitable shales were found early in the seventeenth century near Guisborough and alum workings were extensive throughout the area traversed by the path, until an easier process was found as a by-product of coal mining. Thereafter the industry shifted from the North Riding to the West Riding to be nearer the source of supply. The abandoned workings may be seen all along the coast, where many formerly prominent headlands have literally been quarried away, and also on the north and west escarpments.

Iron was worked in the Middle Ages from local deposits, including deposits at Rievaulx Abbey, and much woodland was felled in this period to provide fuel for the smelting furnaces. Rich seams were found also near Guisborough in the middle of the nineteenth century and it was these deposits that led to industrial development on Tees-side. The ores are no longer economic compared with imported ore, but much damage was done to the landscape during working, though fortunately outside the immediate area covered by the long distance path, from which, however, considerable evidence of the industry can be seen.

The limestone deposits are well suited to building and many of the houses in the villages at the foot of the moors have been constructed from it. Today the limestone is mainly quarried and crushed for use as agricultural lime.

Romans, Angles and Normans

The moors have never been heavily populated, the various peoples coming to the area having chosen to found their settlements in the richer land below the moors rather than on their barren tops. There were, however, Neolithic and Bronze Age settlements, though few in number, and some dykes, barrows and earthworks will be seen, particularly on promontory sites which, here as elsewhere, were no doubt attractive to isolated tribes for their defence advantages. York was an important Roman centre and a well-preserved section of Roman road, Wade's Causeway, lies within the moorland area and the national park, but the only other significant sites with Roman associations near the path are the Roman signalling stations along the coast. These were intended to keep watch over the shores which were vulnerable to the marauding Germanic tribes who were on the move all over Europe towards the end of the Roman era. A comparison with the present-day anti-missile early warning station on Fylingdales Moor is inevitable.

The Angles, who chose this area for settlement, approached the moors both from the sea and from the Vale of Pickering, and have left particular evidence of their presence in the many placenames along the route ending in '-ley' or '-ton', eg Helmsley, Carlton, Cloughton, Ayton, Stokesley, Osmotherley. The Danes, who came later, left their own legacy of placenames, mostly ending in '-by', eg Ingleby, Easby, Faceby, Swainby and Whitby; and in such forms as the various Nabs, Scars and Wykes along the path.

In later, Norman, times the upland areas of moor continued to discourage settlement except for scattered farms, and they became the appurtenance of religious houses and of rich families as well as common land for villagers who preferred to site their villages in more sheltered places. The organisation and industry of the religious foundations secured for them an important place in the simple economy of their day and they flourished with the many gifts from the local lords of what was to them useless land. Even after the dissolution of the monasteries the influence of Roman Catholicism remained, and remains, strong among the landowning classes in the area, and Ampleforth, the well-known Roman Catholic public school, was founded here. The ruins of the religious houses are significant points of interest along the route. The area has remained wild and lonely to this day in spite of the roads constructed in recent times, the advent of the motor car and increased leisure to use it. Along the coast sheltered bays in later centuries favoured the growth of fishing villages, now mostly holiday resorts, and there are also old and now extensive urban areas on the route at Whitby and Scarborough. The chief use of the moors seen from the path is, and always has been, sheep-grazing, though extensive afforestation with conifers has taken place since World War I, much of it to the detriment of the traditional landscape. In some cases early plantations along the slopes of the moor edge, now mature, obscure the view outwards from the path.

Vegetation and Scenery

The dominant vegetation on the moor is heather and bracken, and fire is always a danger, though the dead heather seen in some places is deliberately burnt to encourage young shoots in the interests of grouse-rearing. The area is not noted for the variety or rarity of its flora but limestone-loving species flourish where this rock occurs. Trees, other than recent plantings, are not a feature of the landscape except in areas of landslip along the scarp and in sheltered dales, having disappeared largely as a result of over-grazing by sheep and rabbits and as a result of felling in the Middle Ages to provide charcoal for iron smelting. There is evidence that the moors were heavily wooded in prehistoric times. Foxes and badgers may be seen but they favour the sheltered dales and it would be unusual to see them on the route, though smaller mammals will be met with. The most commonly seen birds are red grouse, curlews and golden plovers as well as the more usual birds of field and hedgerow; along the coast herring gulls, cormorants and kittiwakes may be seen.

Curlew

The main characteristic of the area traversed by the path is its peace and quiet and sense of openness and space, for it has not as yet become a tourist area on a national scale, most visitors coming from the local industrial areas of Tees-side. The walker on the Moors Path will most likely have to come down off the hills for accommodation to market towns such as Thirsk, Stokesley and Guisborough or to villages such as Faceby, Swainby and Ingleby Greenhow, where he will find much of visual and historic interest. On the Coast Path the problem of accommodation is likely to be less pressing because of the many holiday towns.

The Route: Helmsley and Ryedale

The *Moors Path* starts in Helmsley as a farm lane leading westwards from the B1257 road almost opposite the church.

Helmsley is a quiet market town in Ryedale with a fine square and an imposing castle, built between 1186 and 1227, now a ruin on a commanding height above the town with a well-preserved keep and massive earthworks. Nearby is Duncombe Park, designed by Vanbrugh and formerly the home of the Earls of Feversham but now a girls' school. There is good accommodation and some attractive old buildings in the town.

The lane peters out and some stiles in open fields are crossed to reach a small wood, the edge of which is followed until the path dips down into a little wooded valley and up along the edge of the wood again to meet a carriage-track, where there is an estate lodge. One is now on Whinny Bank high above the winding River Rye, looking across the valley to where little streams fall down the lower wooded slopes on the opposite bank. The track joins a road down to the bridge across the Rye, where a few hundred yards to the north are the ruins of Rievaulx Abbey. This Cistercian house was founded in 1132 in an area chosen for its isolation and solitude, the order's rule being so severe that the monks destroyed a village one and a half miles away when the abbey was built. The canals constructed to link the site with the River Rye for the transport of building materials are still extant.

The path ascends Nettledale, in which is one of the tributaries of the River Rye, passing through Forestry Commission land, where it is necessary to take care that the right route is taken. The route turns up

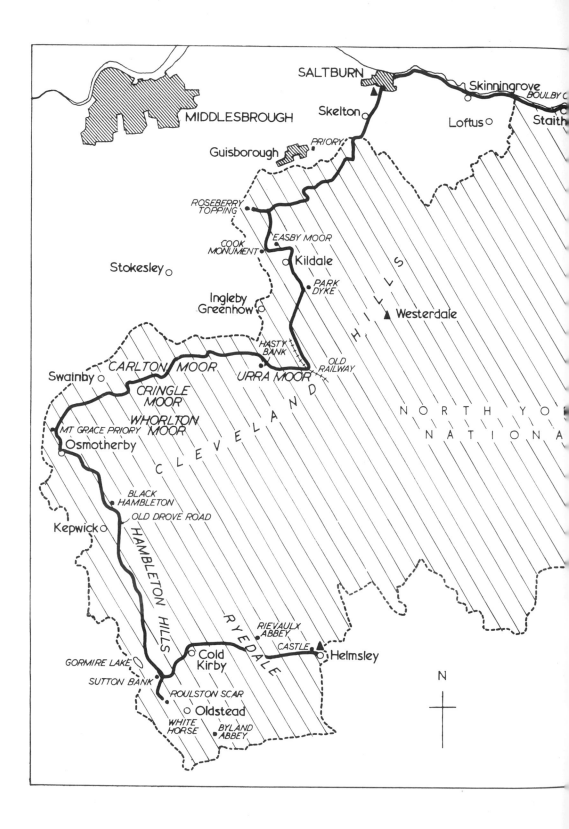

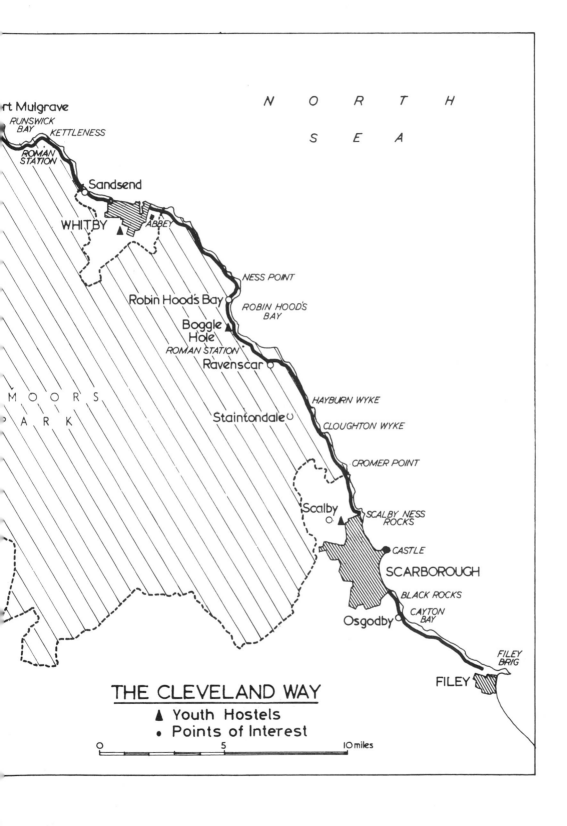

N O R T H

S E A

rt Mulgrave
RUNSWICK BAY
KETTLENESS
ROMAN STATION
Sandsend
WHITBY ▲ *ABBEY*

NESS POINT

Robin Hood's Bay ○
ROBIN HOOD'S BAY

Boggle Hole ▲
ROMAN STATION
Ravenscar ○

HAYBURN WYKE

M O O R S
P A R K

Staintondale ○
CLOUGHTON WYKE

CROMER POINT

Scalby ○ ▲
SCALBY NESS ROCKS
● *CASTLE*

SCARBOROUGH
BLACK ROCKS
CAYTON BAY
Osgodby ○

FILEY BRIG
FILEY

THE CLEVELAND WAY
▲ Youth Hostels
● Points of Interest

0 _____ 5 _____ 10 miles

Flassendale and comes out of it almost immediately by a small side valley to the north. A lane leads from the top of the dale across an open plateau to the village of Cold Kirby and past Hambleton House, a racing establishment, to the A170 where there is an inn but no accommodation. You have now a choice of going westwards along the road a short distance and then alongside an old dyke direct to Sutton Bank where there is a view which seems to stretch endlessly across the tidy fields in the Vale of York below, or of making the short detour south by a metalled track to Roulston Scar. The White Horse of Kilburn is cut in the south-facing scarp-face below. It is not an ancient monument, the whitewashed figure having been contrived by a local schoolmaster in 1857, but it is now a symbol and landmark for the whole area. Here also there are panoramic views across the plains to south and west. The path then curves back along the moor edge to Sutton Bank, from which the Yorkshire Gliding Club operates, and down which a very steep road runs.

Sutton Bank and Black Hambleton

From Sutton Bank (or from Roulston Scar, if the detour is made) the path follows the high edge of the North York Moors National Park over the Hambleton and Cleveland Hills, with wide views to the west over the hedgerows and farmsteads of the plains of York and Mowbray to the

Gormire Lake from Sutton Bank
(*J Allan Cash Ltd*)

Pennines on the skyline or, in the north, across the Tees valley. The path from Sutton Bank overlooks Gormire Lake (see opposite), which has been formed by ice action on the débris of an ancient landslip, and leads to the vertical limestone crags of Whitestone Cliff, where a bridleway is joined. This continues along the edge above the tree-covered limestone slopes past the Iron Age fort and ditch at Boltby Scar to join the Hambleton drove road at High Paradise. This old green road is part of a very much longer route formerly used by Scottish and Northumbrian drovers to bring cattle to the markets in the south-east. Beyond the roadside stump of Steeple Cross (crosses were often set up at road junctions) and the ruins of Limekiln House, formerly an inn for drovers, the drove road approaches Black Hambleton itself, where there are now long views eastwards across the heather moors.

We skirt the western side of Black Hambleton and drop to the head of Oakdale. The way down Oakdale to Osmotherley can be difficult to follow in the high summer because of the tall bracken. The path keeps close to the stream as far as the reservoir and crosses a stone bridge over a feeder stream north of the reservoir. There is then a short climb in a north-west direction to pick up a grass track which soon meets the road down to Osmotherley. This small market town provides refreshment and accommodation and has at its centre an interesting cross and a large stone table which has been used for such varied purposes as a resting place for corpses, a market stall and a pulpit for John Wesley.

Osmotherley to Carlton Moor

North of Osmotherley the Cleveland Hills begin and the first feature of interest on the route after climbing Ruebury Hill on to the moor is the Lady Chapel, now part of a farmhouse. The chapel, built early in the sixteenth century, was restored last century for private use by the landowner. At the foot of the steep hillside, fringed with trees, lie the ruins of Mount Grace Priory, but it is difficult of access from this quarter and is best approached by road from Osmotherley. This Carthusian monastery, founded in 1398 by the Duke of Surrey, provided an austere living for the monks until the dissolution in 1539, each monk having his own stone cell, to which was attached a garden in which he worked alone, their discipline imposing strict rules of silence and isolation.

The path continues as a wide track with a wall on the left and Forestry Commission plantations below, towards Scarth Nick, a gap in the hills gouged out during the Ice Age, where there are good views to the north. Across the cattle grid the road going down to the village of Swainby is a continuation of the Hambleton drove road, which we descend through Clain Wood to a point overlooking the valley of Scugdale Beck. Some signs of old workings for jet, sandstone and limestone may be seen here. Swainby was settled at the time of the Black Death from Whorlton just a little to the east, where the remains of the castle and church still stand.

The path changes direction and follows the hill round, gradually approaching the pleasant beck in its steep-sided valley and crossing the stream by a ford. On the other side of the fertile valley we ascend gently at first, and then sharply up a track to Knolls End and Whorlton Moor where the detached knoll of Whorlton Hill stands up out of the lower ground to the left. Several miles further on above Faceby Bank we come through heather moor to Carlton Moor where a road comes up steeply from the village of Carlton. From this height the views across the wide patchwork of the plain to the north and west are spectacular and in the autumn the purple heather and the brown of the dying bracken make a magnificent display of colour. Here also, however, the buildings and equipment of the Newcastle Gliding Club are prominent on the hill-top; gliding may be seen on summer weekends, as at Roulston Scar at the beginning of the route. On the slopes up to the moor the small spoil heaps can be seen dotted about where adits were driven in for the underground working of jet. There are also signs of the alum workings which were abandoned here at the end of the eighteenth century. Alongside the path some burial mounds can be seen, including the remains of some with hollow tops, indicating that they have been plundered for treasure.

Hasty Bank to Kildale

Between here and Hasty Bank three miles to the east the path crosses the rounded tops of Cringle Moor (where the highest point is crowned by Drake Howe tumulus) and Cold Moor, both made resplendent with heather, bilberry, crowberry and the tough moorland grasses, but there are also some wet and difficult stretches of bog with sphagnum, cotton grass and thick-growing bracken. At their best in summer and autumn when the moors are ablaze with colour, these hills can be dark and grim in winter. Hasty Bank is one of the finest viewpoints along the whole route. When work was carried out on the construction of the popular car park at the site in 1970 numerous bones were found, the remains of burials made in the Bronze Age.

From Hagg's Gate the route ascends steeply to Urra Moor, past what

Bonny Cliff towards Carlton Bank, from Cringle Moor (*Crown Copyright*)

may be a prehistoric dyke, and follows the ruin of the great glacial re-entrant of Greenhow Bolton, which cuts deeply into the moor at this point. The climb is steep along a forestry wall. Many of the slopes in this area have been planted with conifers since the war, and the expanses of dark green woodland with regular edges, though pleasant in themselves, detract from the sweep and continuity of the moors, and sometimes hide the views. But at the top of Urra Moor one can, at 1,500ft, stand on the highest point of the North York Moors with commanding views of Bilsdale stretching away to the south and, in the other direction, across Greenhow Bolton to the hills that one will be walking on in a short time. The track, still across open moor, eventually joins a metalled road but first follows a short section of the track of a remarkable old railway which used to carry iron ore to Middlesbrough and which plunged incredibly down the precipitous scarp to the west on its way to the plain. The path continues along the moor edge, which it leaves by a green track that drops down round Park Nab to the village of Kildale. Park Nab may be climbed to the ancient earthwork on its top, and it is possible to approach Park Dyke, of uncertain origin, which runs parallel to the route on the open ground on the right. In Kildale, which has one small shop but no accommodation, is the site of an old manor house that once belonged to the Percy family.

Gorse

The Cook Monument and Roseberry Topping

North of Kildale the stone obelisk of Captain Cook's monument, which is a prominent landmark in the area, lies a short distance away on Easby Moor not far from Airy Holme Farm to the north-west under Roseberry Topping, where Captain Cook spent part of his boyhood. The route passes the monument and includes a short spur to Roseberry Topping, an isolated conical hill capped with gritstone and with terraced slopes due to the alternation of adjacent beds of harder and softer rocks. There are some boggy patches on the next sections of Hutton and Guisborough Moors where the headwaters of south-flowing streams are crossed. We are now entering an area which has been severely marked by former ironstone and alum working, the alum working having started here as early as Elizabethan times. The path overlooks Guisborough and the walker may wish to visit this town to see the remains of the Augustinian priory founded by a member of the Scottish Bruce family in 1120.

The path descends past a rifle range and forestry land to the A171 Guisborough–Whitby road, through very extensive quarry workings at Slapewath, crosses the road near the Fox and Hounds Inn and continues along the edge which is considerably lower now than on the heights of the Cleveland Hills as the scarp peters out towards Skelton. From here it is a short walk down over fields and under the railway viaduct to the municipal gardens in the valley of Skelton Beck and into the seaside town of Saltburn, where the Moors Path ends and the Coast Path begins.

Saltburn to Whitby

The *Coast Path* starts at the cliff track which climbs up from Old Saltburn near the Ship Inn. Throughout its length it keeps close to the cliff-edge, to Whitby and Scarborough and beyond, for some forty miles. In parts the cliffs are subject to subsidence due to the friable rocks and soft boulder clay of which they are made, and they are steep, so attention is needed, though there is no real danger if reasonable care is taken. There is great pleasure to be derived from following the winding path with seemingly endless views across great expanses of empty sea or looking down at the skirting of jagged reefs or tumbled cliff débris with encroaching vegetation at the cliff foot, or of observing the changing colours and textures of the rock strata or the swooping flight of the sea-birds. But there is also interest on the land side as well. At Huntcliffe, outside Saltburn, for example, is the site of the first of five Roman signalling stations along this coast, built in the fourth century AD to warn of Anglian and Saxon pirates. Each consisted of a high tower protected by a wall and ditch, and no doubt housed a garrison able to pass messages to land and sea forces stationed elsewhere.

The route then takes the walker along the coast and down the soft low cliff to the sands in front of Skinningrove, where vast ironworks tower above like grim medieval castles. These incongruous structures appear unreal in what is otherwise a beautiful and natural landscape. An old railway line curves along the coast between Saltburn and Skinningrove and continues to loop its way along the coastal belt, now skirting the cliff edge, now veering sharply away from it. This line was used to take away steel products, alum, ironstone, fish and agricultural produce to the Middlesbrough area. The path makes use of the old track later on.

After Skinningrove the path passes along the top of Boulby Cliffs, at 666ft the highest in England, in an area where halfway down on the cliff shelf ironstone, alum and jet have all been worked. It drops down into Staithes (see opposite), a picturesque fishing village of dark stone and slate squeezed into a narrow glacial valley with high walls on either side. Its main street plunges down the 'bank' to a tiny grey harbour with fishermen's cottages, and its narrow and twisted streets have houses piled

Boulby from just outside Loftus
(*Crown Copyright*)

one above the other. Captain Cook was apprenticed to a grocer in Staithes in the middle 1700s.

Port Mulgrave is no more than a few miners' cottages but below is the tiny harbour from which ironstone was once exported. The path then passes the site of Lingrove Howe long barrow into Runswick Bay, a bright and popular holiday village with whitewashed buildings and red tile roofs. Here it is best to take the sands eastwards towards Kettleness and avoid the slippery, channelled boulder clay above it until this has to be tackled up the slopes of one of the streams in order to regain the cliff-top. There are further very extensive ironstone, alum and jet workings at Kettleness and indeed the original 'Ness' is said to have been quarried almost completely away. The Romans took advantage of the headland for the second signalling station but the site is a little way back from the path on the highest ground. The railway line ran close to the Ness for the easier transport of the quarried materials, but it then runs into a mile-long tunnel, reappearing beneath the cliff face at Deepgrove Wyke. We climb down to the track where it emerges from the tunnel and follow it for another mile right through the old workings which here also have moved vast quantities of the cliff face in the course of time. We can now see the alum quarry at close quarters while the natural views out to sea remain no less pleasant from the edge of the track. At Sandsend the old railway track and the road run close together along the shore edge. The beach may be used into Whitby, or the road can be taken past the golf course, returning to the coast over the footbridge and under the railway at Upgang and thus into Whitby.

Whitby to Filey

There is much of interest in the old town of Whitby, including the monastery (see page 98) founded in AD657 by St Hilda of Northumbria to celebrate a victory over the Mercians, the ruins of which are alongside the route. The monastery was sacked by the Danes in AD867, rebuilt after the Norman Conquest and abandoned at the dissolution in 1539. It continued to serve as a landmark to sailors, however, the structure always

Whitby Abbey

in danger of collapse because of the exposure of the site to the elements. At the Synod of Whitby in AD664 the English Church turned away from the practices of the Celtic to those of the Roman Church. The town has a strong atmosphere, with stone buildings, red roofs, and a harbour well filled with fishing vessels.

From the abbey the path goes along East Cliff, past the black shale headland of Saltwick Nab and the caravan site at Saltwick Bay to the lighthouse at Whitestone Point. The fine length of coast (some twenty miles) between Whitby and Scarborough exposes a great variety of cliff forms as the various strata of shales, clays, sandstones and limestones rise to the surface with their different colouring. Where the softer clays in the lias reach the surface they have, as at Robin Hood's Bay, been eroded away leaving extensive reefs of hard rock exposed on the seabed; the bay is three miles across from North Cheek to South Cheek. The limestone cliffs are often near-vertical while the clay produces more rounded forms, and great boulders lie strewn at the bottom of the sandstone cliffs. The area is noted for the wealth of fossils found embedded in the rocks.

Robin Hood's Bay village is perched high on top of limestone cliffs, the red-roofed houses set at angles to each other, while Ravenscar is spread out in regular lines away from the cliff at the south end of the bay at South Cheek. The village looks half finished, a ground-work of streets having been laid out as part of a planned development which was never realised. At that time a large hotel was built on the cliffs covering the site of another Roman signalling station. In approaching the settlement the path comes slightly inland across a curious narrow plateau between the coast and a scarp edge half a mile back from the cliff (this scarp was also extensively worked for alum) in order to avoid the steep-sided gills which cut into the coast at right angles. At Hayburn Wyke, further on still, a stream is crossed by a footbridge in a steep-sided valley, where there are pleasant woods and an attractive waterfall. There is only one further indentation on this straight coastline before Scarborough is reached, at Cloughton Wyke where one can look from the 100ft cliffs to where the sea swirls among the sandstone rocks.

After Scarborough the path continues, now well outside the national park, towards Filey. The cliffs are lower and there are many signs of development at first in the form of bungalows and caravan sites, and one is always conscious of the main road, which runs at but a short distance from the coast. But at Lebberston and Gristhorpe Cliffs there is much of natural and scenic interest, particularly in the offshore reefs and in the formation of the cliffs themselves with their layered rocks topped with crumbling boulder clay. The path ends at the county boundary before reaching Filey, but the walker will certainly wish to continue to the town, past the mile-long oolite reef of Filey Brigg, which besides being a natural curiosity acts as a ready-made barrier and protection for the town.

8 · The South Downs Way

Opened: 15 July 1972

Length: 80 miles (129km)

A Long Distance Bridleway

The South Downs Way, 129km (80 miles) long, is the first and only long distance bridleway, ie the only route which is open to horse-riders throughout its length. There is, however, an additional section of the route along the high cliffs between Eastbourne and the Cuckmere valley which is not suitable for riders and is available only to walkers. All the rest of the route can be used by walkers as well as riders, and they do in fact make up the greater number of users. Cyclists may also use the bridleway route.

The ridge of the South Downs has been used as a means of communication from the earliest times. Like the other chalk ridges in southern England (the North Downs and the chalkland extending from the Wash to the Berkshire and Marlborough Downs and beyond) the South Downs ridge offered a dry causeway well above the dark and humid forests of the surrounding clay plains. These ridge routes provided a convenient entry point for the nomadic tribes who peopled Britain from various starting points on the Continent in Neolithic, Bronze Age and Iron Age times, and all three ridges meet in Salisbury Plain, where the Neolithic peoples set up their religious centre at Stonehenge. The trackways which they first marked out are bordered throughout their length with ample evidence of their passage, burial places of various shapes and types, stone circles, hill-forts and encampments, 'strip lynchets' (the marks left by early cultivation), dykes, ditches and various earthworks for boundary demarcation and defence—culminating in the mysterious and impressive architecture of Avebury and Stonehenge.

When stock-rearing became a viable agricultural practice the short rich grass of the chalk encouraged the keeping of flocks of sheep and the South Downs were so used in historic times in turn by Celtic, Roman, Saxon and Norman settlers all of whom have in other ways left their marks on the area. Indeed it is only since World War II that new farming methods have led to extensive enclosure for arable farming, and the virtual elimination of sheep. During this period, lasting over many centuries, the track on the crest of the downs continued to serve a useful purpose as a drove road for stock. It is only in the twentieth century that the ridge track has entered a new phase in its long history, this time to serve the leisure needs of an urban and industrialised population.

The South Downs was proposed as a national park by the Hobhouse Committee on National Parks, but the reduction in potential access land due to enclosure for ploughing argued against this and all the land in which the South Downs Way lies has instead been designated as areas of outstanding natural beauty. Sheep-grazing areas do nevertheless occur and areas of open country still exist, scrub tending to invade those tracts from which sheep have been withdrawn.

Geology and Scenery

Geologically the South Downs are the lower sides of a great fold or anticline whose apex was formerly above the Weald, and which consisted of bands of chalk, greensand and clay in successive layers. The upper part of the fold has been drastically worn down over time by erosion, so that the Weald is now a depression, and the northward-facing edge of chalk is the South Downs, while the southward-facing edge is the North Downs. Between these two edges the Weald, where the lower layers of sand and clay are now at the surface, produces a different kind of natural landscape, mainly heathland and oak woods. Apart from Forest Ridges, however, this woodland has largely been cut down, not only for agriculture but, during the seventeenth and eighteenth centuries, for shipbuilding and to provide charcoal for iron-smelting. There are extensive views across the Weald landscape along the whole length of the South Downs Way. The downs themselves are typically bare of trees, but parts of the South Downs Way to the west are nevertheless heavily wooded, due to local deposits of clay with flints overlying the chalk.

The typical landscape is of bare, rounded hills, one succeeding the other, with steep-sided valleys and headlands sweeping down smoothly into the plain of the Weald. These north-facing valleys are often too steep for cultivation, while the gentler slopes on the other side of the ridge are either grassland or large cultivated fields, their light brown or whitish soil displaying in spring numerous round nodules of flint. These flints were themselves an attraction to Neolithic man, and flint mines have been found where the nodules were broken on site to fashion the sharp edges of arrows and other cutting implements. In historic times the flints have provided useful building material and they can often be seen in churches and other buildings near the path, where the stones have been set in cement to make rugged exterior walls. Other buildings in the area, however, reflect in their brick and wooden exteriors the materials that are more readily available in the Weald.

It is a characteristic of chalk that rainwater quickly percolates the soil and underlying rock, and is not retained on the surface, so that water, both for animals and people, is scarce. Most of the small downland valleys are dry, that is, they carry no streams. This has led, so far as water for animals is concerned, to the construction of dew-ponds, many examples of which will be seen along the South Downs Way. Dew-ponds are depressions or excavated areas lined with clay which catch and retain whatever precipitation is available (including dew), so that water collects even where there is no rain, giving rise to the belief that dew-ponds never

Fieldfare

run dry. So far as people are concerned the lack of water has meant that houses are relatively scarce on the downs, the villages having been built lower down where the chalk meets the impervious clay and the water emerges in the form of springs. A whole succession of such villages and hamlets is strung out at the foot of the downs, apparently unchanged for centuries, with Saxon or Norman churches and venerable old dwellings. It is these villages and those in the river valleys that the long distance bridleway user will look to for accommodation, for there are no villages on the downs themselves. Associated with these old villages there are occasional historic mansions with extensive parkland, some of which are open to the public.

The route is cut by a succession of major north–south valleys, which divide the path naturally into sections, and in which run the Cuckmere, the Ouse, the Adur and the Arun rivers. These wide valleys and their meadow-lands set off by the surrounding low hills are of great beauty when looked down upon from the route on the downs, but the slowly winding rivers themselves are not particularly impressive. Their sluggish waters often have a brownish appearance and are hemmed in by high banks set up to protect the valley plains from flooding. At these openings in the downs, where road transport is easier, extensive quarries have sometimes been cut in the hill faces, and there are numerous small chalk-pits elsewhere where the material has been taken for spreading on the heavier soils of the Weald in order to lighten it. Sand pits occur at the western end of the route below the hills in the Rother valley.

Few Difficulties

Walking on the downs presents few difficulties, broad and well used tracks which have been used for centuries making up the greater part of the route. Sometimes there are double, broad tracks, however, and a track will sometimes split into two tracks which gradually diverge. The paths are signposted and waymarked with the acorn symbol but the low-set plinth type of sign used on open downland can easily be overlooked and the landscape should always be carefully read and followed with reference to the line of the route on a map. It is also worth remembering that dry grass and wet chalk on steep slopes can be slippery.

The route can also be reached by car at frequent points, not only at the main road crossings but along minor roads or sunken lanes which lead up the face of the downs and then stop. The local authorities have adopted a policy of constructing small parking spaces well out of sight below the crests of the hills, and from these the public may ascend to make excursions along the South Downs Way, or simply to enjoy the view. These access points, which are useful for taking the long distance bridleway user down to the villages, can be picked out from the map.

Although the route is designed with the needs of riders in mind and particularly the need for good visibility at road crossings, care is still needed by riders at the busier crossings, especially where larger groups of horses and riders are concerned. Accommodation for horses and riders is provided at many of the inns on or near the route and as this is riding country stabling is available. Application can be made to the Countryside Commission for a list of addresses. The Society of Sussex Downsmen has worked to ensure that the route is well maintained and signposted, and has carried out voluntary work on the paths.

The Seven Sisters, Sussex, looking towards Birling Gap (*Leonard and Marjory Gayton*)

The Route: Eastbourne to Cuckmere

The footpath section of the *South Downs Way* begins at the west end of the seafront in Eastbourne, leaving the road where it makes its first sharp bend northwards, and climbing up the well-used path over the turf and through the scrub to reach very quickly a height of 450ft on the way to Beachy Head.

Soon, just past the hotel and the police station on the coast road, one can look down carefully over the vertical chalk cliffs on to the red and white lighthouse, which appears tiny on the rocks 430ft below. The cliffs are liable to break away along this coast and the heights are dizzy, but the path itself is well back from the edge. A mile further on is the Belle Tout Lighthouse, built in 1831 and replaced in 1901 by the one we have just passed. It lies just inside an ancient banked enclosure, the greater part of which has long since disappeared into the sea.

At Birling Gap a cliff fall forces the path temporarily inland to the road and then through the bungalows that make up this cliff-top settlement, while the road itself, which has followed the coastline closely and made it accessible to scores of visitors, disappears northwards towards Eastdean. The path continues along the switchback of the Seven Sisters, in reality the valleys and separating ridges of old dry rivers, before dropping down to the stony beach at Cuckmere Haven at the mouth of the winding Cuckmere River. 700 acres of the downland overlooking the river on the near side, up to the Seaford–Eastbourne road, have been made into a country park. The path, however, passes alongside the caravan site on the popular beach to pick up the flood embankment along the 'cut' which straightens out the huge meanders of the river and follows it up to the main road at Exceat Bridge.

The white cliffs between Cuckmere and Eastbourne along which we have passed are the abrupt eastern extremity of the South Downs. The chalk then passes under the sea to reappear on the French coast, but at one time the land masses were unbroken and it was no doubt across this causeway that the earliest settlers entered to make their way along the chalk ridgeway to Stonehenge, to Avebury and beyond. Today this length of cliff-top offers one of the few extensive areas of undeveloped coastline until as far west as Studland in Dorset. Much of the downland and cliff-top adjacent to Eastbourne has been acquired by Eastbourne Corporation for protection against development, and much of the rest belongs to the National Trust.

Back along the Eastbourne road the path enters the gate of Exceat Farm and climbs across the hill to Westdean, a village where King Alfred, no doubt attracted by the Cuckmere as a harbour for his fleet, is said to have had a palace, though no site is known. It is then a matter of curving round the hillside past the woods and parallel to the river to Charlston Manor and to Litlington. But before the path takes us into Alfriston the tiny Lullington Church is worth a visit; set on its own among trees it is only 16ft square and holds twenty people. We can now cross the wooden bridge over the Cuckmere, much narrower now, and pass along a very narrow lane into the main part of the village. Alfriston is a pretty place and popular with summer visitors. Among the things worth looking at are St Andrew's Church, so large it is called 'the cathedral of the downs'; the pre-Reformation Priest's House, which was bought and restored by the National Trust in 1896 and was its first acquisition; and the Star Inn, which is easily recognised by the ship's figurehead outside, a link with smuggling activity in the eighteenth century from ships calling at Cuckmere Haven.

Alfriston to the Ouse

At Alfriston the footpath section coming from the Seven Sisters joins the main bridleway route coming from Eastbourne. This starts at Pashley, at a point a mile further along the road from which the footpath started, or alternatively the downs can be climbed from the quieter road leading directly up the hill from the golf course. The bridle track then skirts the edge of the downs northwards, with Eastbourne spread out below on our right, but instead of continuing along the edge we bear left over to Willingdon Hill and down again to Jevington village. We then cross the road to the lane that leads past the stone and flint Saxon Church of St Andrew and make the steady climb to Windover Hill, also over 600ft, and down to join the footpath route at Alfriston. Windover Hill is on the edge of the downs and gives us our first significant view northwards over the Weald. It has an Iron Age site on its top and on the hill face is cut the celebrated 270ft-long Long Man of Wilmington. The figure, which carries a staff in each hand and is now marked out with white bricks, looks down on the site of Wilmington Priory whose monks are thought to have cut the first outline some time after its foundation in the eleventh century.

The seven miles from Alfriston to the Ouse valley include all the main features that characterise the downs and the South Downs Way—distant views on either hand, sweeps of hillside and dry valleys, tumuli, dewponds, great fields with post and wire fencing instead of hedges, and a clear track interrupted only by the occasional gate and rising modestly to a higher point from time to time. The high points are all over 600ft, Bostal Hill and Beddingham Hill with, in the middle, Firle Beacon rising to a height of 713ft and providing a magnificent viewpoint to as far away as the North Downs. The Beacon was used as a signalling site at the time of the Armada; Beddingham Hill now has a ring of tall masts. Just below the Beacon is Firle Place and its extensive park, the home of the Gage family. The mansion is largely eighteenth century but incorporates a Tudor house. Beyond it, at the foot of a great outlier of the downs and below Mount Caburn which with its Iron Age fort crowns the outlier, is the Elizabethan mansion and park of Glynde Place. Both houses are open to the public at advertised times, though the long distance walker may have to forgo a visit since most of the route still lies ahead. It is even less likely that he can spare the time to visit Glyndebourne, the country house and mansion with opera-house attached which lies only slightly further away and out of sight from the hills. These opportunities are open to the motorist, however, who can also gain some impression of the South Downs Way, for a number of small roads lead up from the A27 to the downland ridge. At Alciston, just below Bo-peep Farm, a carefully-sited parking place has been constructed by the East Sussex County Council at the bottom of the downs to encourage such visits.

The path descends Itford Hill to Itford Farm and enters the road opposite the farm to cross the main railway line and the flat flood-plain of the Ouse. Horse-riders should exercise care in crossing the railway line; red and green lights have been installed for their safety. They must use the bridle gates fitted alongside the level crossing gates, having first satisfied themselves that no trains are approaching. It is possible to telephone to the nearest signal box for this purpose. It is important to avoid a situation where numbers of horses and riders are trapped between the gates and unable to get out in time when a train is coming. Pedestrians can use the footbridge. The river is crossed by a large iron swing-bridge, which was originally put up as a farm access but which became so heavily used as an alternative to the busier crossings at Newhaven and Lewes that its stability was threatened and the road had to be closed to vehicular traffic.

Southease to the Adur

At Southease we pass a fine Norman church (see right) on the left, with a rare example of a round flint tower. Riders should again be careful in emerging on to the busy A275 from Lewes to Newhaven as visibility is restricted on the right, and in following the A275 to Rodmell, where the road verges should be used.

From the lane at Rodmell, once the home of Leonard and Virginia Woolf, we climb up to the downs again at Mill Hill, followed by Iford Hill and Swanborough Hill, both rising to over 600ft and overlooking Kingston and Lewes in one direction and giving views across the farmed downland to the sea in the other. The track across the bare and open downland has more examples of dew-ponds and tumuli. It joins the old drove road and fishermen's track, Jugg's road, coming up from Kingston, which we leave to follow a fence round the head of a great steep-sided coombe to meet another broad track at Newmarket Plantation which we follow straight down in the opposite direction to the A27 at Newmarket Inn, about halfway between Brighton and Lewes.

Southease Church

Through a gate on the opposite side of the road the bridleway makes a wide sweep up and across the downland west of Lewes, meeting the scarp again above the village of Plumpton near Black Cap. On the downland in the direction of Lewes away to our right the Battle of Lewes took place in 1264. Henry III's cavalry under Prince Edward impetuously pursued Simon de Montfort's men, who had temporarily broken, up on to the downs, but de Montfort was able to rally and to call on reserves so that the

The South Downs Way, south-west of Lewes

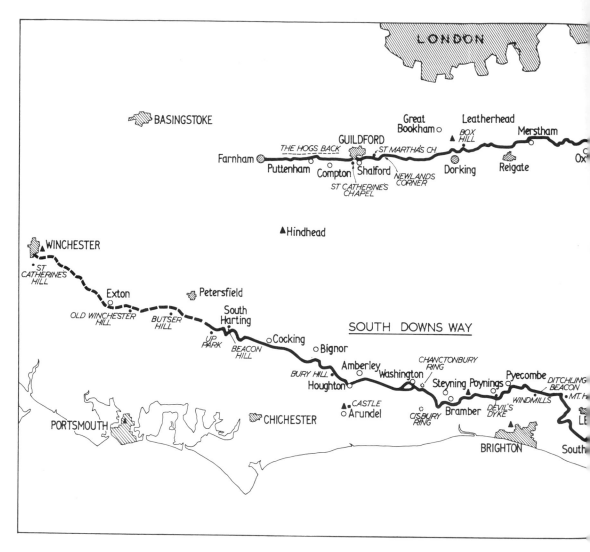

king's division was in the end defeated. Many of the fleeing troops were drowned in the marshes of the Ouse valley, which is now dyked and drained but was then liable to flooding.

Now firmly back on the edge of the downs again the path continues unswervingly along the high ground towards the gap at Pyecombe followed by the A23. This is one of the best parts of the downland and the views across the peaceful countryside are magnificent, as we pass by Plumpton Plain, Street Hill and Western Brow to the outstanding viewpoint, and the highest point on the route, at Ditchling Beacon (813ft). The Beacon has an Iron Age camp and was also the site of an Armada signalling station. Slowly descending from the Beacon, after about a mile we come to a metalled lane where we see the twin windmills, Jack and Jill. Jill, built in 1821, was transported from Patcham near Brighton in 1850, and Jack was added in 1876. But we veer left to avoid using the enclosed lane and then right along the edge of Pyecombe golf

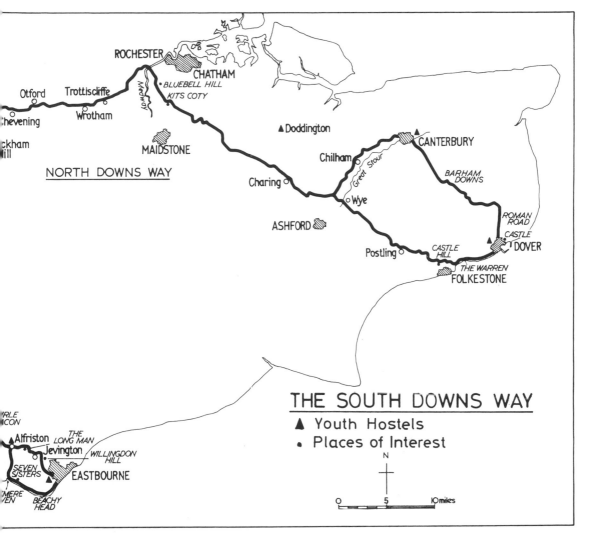

Map labels:

ROCHESTER
CHATHAM
BLUEBELL HILL
KITS COTY
Otford
Trottiscliffe
Wrotham
Chevening
ckham
ill
Medway
MAIDSTONE
NORTH DOWNS WAY
▲ Doddington
Chilham
Great Stour
CANTERBURY
BARHAM DOWNS
Charing
Wye
ROMAN ROAD
CASTLE
ASHFORD
CASTLE HILL
DOVER
Postling
THE WARREN
FOLKESTONE

THE SOUTH DOWNS WAY
▲ Youth Hostels
• Places of Interest

N

RLE CON
Alfriston
THE LONG MAN
Jevington
WILLINGDON HILL
SEVEN SISTERS
EASTBOURNE
MERE EN
BEACHY HEAD

0   5   10 miles

course to the road (riders should again take care on coming on to the road). The railway is in a tunnel under the high downs and the strange structures near the clubhouse are ventilation shafts. Pyecombe is tiny; last century it had a great reputation for making shepherds' crooks.

The path leaves out the projecting downland scarp at Newtimber Hill, climbing up from the inn on the A23 past Haresdeane Farm and across farmed downland to West Hill and down to Saddlescombe Farm, once in the ownership of the Knights Templar. We now follow small roads, or the open land just off them, to the Devil's Dyke. The Devil started cutting his dyke to let the sea flood through the downs into the Weald, where there were too many churches for his liking. But an old woman, made curious by the noise, lit a candle and wakened the cocks so that the Devil was frustrated, because the job had to be finished before dawn (which he thought had arrived). Apart from the great natural cleft of the dyke, there are to be seen the Iron Age fortifications on Dyke Hill alongside. There

Twin windmills, Jack and Jill

Riders on the South Downs Way
in winter (*Crown Copyright*)

are tremendous views and there is a hotel where refreshments may be had. The area has been popular with Brighton residents since Victorian times when in addition to the hotel there was a railway linking the Devil's Dyke and the town, a funicular railway across the dyke and amusements which attracted thousands. A proposal to rebuild the hotel and revive these activities, to set up a zoo and introduce modern entertainments, including the building of a replica of the Egyptian temple of Abu Simbel, was refused planning permission after a public inquiry in the 1960s.

Edburton Hill has its ancient encampment, but neither from here nor from Truleigh Hill can we enjoy the views, for the path runs behind both hills. At Truleigh Hill there were, until recently, the masts and miscellaneous buildings of a wartime radar station, but these have been cleared away and we pass alongside brick farm buildings to Tottington Barn. This building was acquired and renovated by the Youth Hostels Association to provide accommodation for users of the long distance bridleway, including riders. We follow the metalled way in front of the hostel to where it forks to Upper Beeding and Shoreham, and take a bridleway leading down to the main road at the bottom of the Adur valley. From here we take a new path leading to a new bridle bridge constructed to take the path across the river to Botolphs and thence up Annington Hill to Steyning Round Hill.

This crossing of the river keeps the path well away from the busy main road through Upper Beeding, Bramber and Steyning. Previously the river crossing was made north of Bramber by an existing bridge in the meadowland between the priory and King's Barn, but the danger from traffic was not entirely avoided. Those stopping off at the aforementioned towns may nevertheless wish to visit the ruins of the Norman castle on the hill-top at Bramber, or to see its interesting museum and its picturesque

The way leading to Chanctonbury Ring (*J Allan Cash Ltd*)

buildings, which include a fifteenth-century timber-fronted house known as St Mary's. Steyning is also a pleasant old market town with old and interesting buildings. In the other direction, a mile off the route towards Worthing, is Cissbury Ring, an outstanding example of a hill-fort where there are the remains of Neolithic flint-mines.

Steyning to the Arun

From Steyning Round Hill the trek along the ridge of the open downs continues for some nine miles to the next break at the Arun valley. The first main point of interest is at Chanctonbury Ring (see above), where at a height of nearly 800ft the present thick ring of beeches was planted in 1760 by Sir Charles Gore of Wiston House, a great Elizabethan mansion which lies just below the downs. The trees enclose in a dark grove the well-preserved embankments of another hill-fort, as well as the remains of two Roman buildings. The ring is a landmark from far and wide and the views from the hill are very extensive.

The path drops down a track to the A24 a mile south of Washington village, and ascends on the other side by Highden Hill. The busy dual carriageway may be crossed directly but if riders are apprehensive an alternative route leads northwards to Washington where the road may be crossed by a bridge and the route rejoined at Barnsfarm Hill.

There follows another fine and open section of the South Downs Way, where it runs for five miles over Kithurst, Springhead and Rackham Hills to Amberley Mount. Below the downs is Parham House, another Elizabethan mansion set in an extensive park where deer graze, which is also open to the public. The route then descends by a large lime quarry to Amberley station. The village is a mile to the north but for those with time it is worth a visit for its manor house, thatched cottages and remains of a fourteenth-century castle.

Up to now the path has traversed grass-covered hill-tops with wide views over the Weald towards the north and, at the foot of the hills, numerous villages and hamlets with ancient churches and timber, flint or brick houses and village greens, which appear to have changed little for hundreds of years. Now, west of the Arun, we enter an area where we still keep to the high ridge, but where the chalk is overlain with sand and clay and there is in consequence thick woodland, particularly on the steeper slopes. Although the countryside itself has not changed materially the views of it are more restricted.

The Arun to Up Park

Having crossed the Arun by the road bridge the path turns right at Houghton village and then left off the road up the slope over fields to Bury Hill, Westburton Hill and Bignor Hill. Just past Bignor Hill there is a point where a large number of paths meet. One of these paths is Stane Street, the Roman road from Chichester to London which we follow for a short distance before it starts its descent of the downs. At Bignor, at the foot of the downs, Bignor Roman Villa was discovered in 1811. Wooden structures with thatched roofs have been built over the exposed foundations, giving some impression of what the farm-cum-villa may have originally looked like. There are some very fine mosaics and the elaborate nature of the extensive buildings may be seen, as well as an exhibition of finds made on the site. The path then continues over Sutton Down and Littleton End to the gap in the downs followed by the A285 at Littleton Farm and carries on to Woolavington Down; in so doing it departs from the true line of the scarp and follows the shortest line where the scarp projects forward to Barlavington.

The South Downs Way could, with advantage, be altered to follow the true line of the scarp round Barlavington Downs, but for the present the scarp edge is picked up again at Graffham Down, where a straight broad track takes us between trees for a long way to Manorfarm Down and the lane at Hill Barn which leads down to the A286 near Cocking. Another lane leads up to the continuation of the track through heavily wooded country straight across Cocking Down and Linch Down to Treyford Hill. Although both slopes are heavily wooded the flat tops of the hills are generally open and have been turned to agricultural use. On the south side of Treyford Hill on Philliswood Down, near the barrows known as the Devil's Jumps, a bridleway turns off and drops down through the trees to the road which goes to Buriton Farm, and on through fields to an old earthwork which is followed to Beacon Hill which is contoured on its southern side. Beacon Hill, too, has been used as a signalling station; it was a station on a semaphore chain leading from Portsmouth to London during the Napoleonic Wars.

A stiff climb brings us to the clear grass track on Harting Down from which there are good views, and to Tower Hill, which is part of the National Trust property of Up Park. The house was built in the Dutch style in 1680 and has associations with Emma, Lady Hamilton, who was brought to live in the house in 1780 by the owner when she was fifteen,

Skylark

long before she met Sir William Hamilton, much less Nelson. The table on which she danced may be seen at the house. H. G. Wells was brought up at the house, where his mother was in service. Trollope lived at South Harting, just down the hill.

Butser Hill and Winchester

The path follows the edge of the park on the slope through the trees and continues across the road by Forty Acre Lane to Sunwood Park. The South Downs Way ends at the Hampshire–Sussex boundary, but there is a proposal to extend it to Winchester. The downland ridge in Hampshire is in general much less well-defined than the preceding sections of downland and the route of the path would therefore determine itself to a much lesser extent. The continuation would be by way of Queen Elizabeth Forest by existing track and thence to the great buttress, and popular country park, of Butser Hill, where there is general access over a wide area and, at 888ft, extensive views. It would continue by forest and field path to Old Winchester Hill, where at 648ft there are also good views and a good example of a hill-fort. From Exton village the route may take a north-west course through a countryside of small woods and intensively used agricultural land to St Catherine's Hill and thence into Winchester.

9 · The North Downs Way

Length: 141 miles (227km)

A Route Close to London

This long distance path runs from Farnham along the entire length of the North Downs in Surrey and Kent to Folkestone, with a branch leading off, where the way meets the River Stour, first along this river valley to Canterbury and then to Dover and finally back along the cliffs to Folkestone. This subsidiary line is a concession to the Pilgrims' Way, with which the North Downs Way is inevitably associated, and takes in some orchard country typical of the 'Garden of England', but its continuation beyond Canterbury as a loop route also creates a shorter, self-contained circular route of some fifty miles. The total distance, including both routes, is 227km (141 miles).

For the greater part of its length the path gives superb views southwards over the Weald of Kent and Sussex. It does not always follow the highest ground, partly because the tops of the downs are often thickly wooded and provide no views and partly because a right of way already existed along the lower slopes of the downs for a great part of the way along the historic and prehistoric tracks which have come to be known as the Pilgrims' Way. The views are nevertheless far-reaching and embrace a landscape of small detail and great historic interest, the same landscape from a different viewpoint that is seen from the South Downs, of which the North Downs are in effect a geological reflection.

The North Downs Way was the second of the great chalk ridgeways to be made into a long distance path, and it shares many of the characteristics of the South Downs Way and of the Ridgeway Path. It has the same short, springy turf and smoothly rounded hill-sides, a soil basically of chalk, a history of sheep-rearing now largely superseded by other uses, villages and great houses strung out along the foot of the downs, buildings incorporating flint, and evidence of use as a highway from very early times. The path is, however, longer than the other two routes, and the hills have rather less bare downland because of the layer of clay with flints that covers the chalk and gives rise to heavy tree growth.

The proximity of a substantial section of the path to the London area makes the North Downs popular for day trips and has also given rise to much scattered residential and other development and a great number of minor roads. Their popularity as a recreation area has caused the county councils, particularly Surrey County Council, to acquire much of the downland as access land and at many places such as Newlands Corner people come in large numbers by car to walk, picnic or simply to enjoy the view. To these areas must be added those owned by the National Trust, as at Colley Hill, Box Hill and Ranmore Common. The whole length of the North Downs has been designated as the Kent and Surrey areas of outstanding natural beauty.

The downs are cut by a number of river valleys, for the rivers, all flowing northward, rise not in the chalk but in the Weald and comprise the Wey, the Mole, the Darenth, the Medway and the Stour. The fact that the rivers cut through the high ground and are not deflected by it suggests that the valleys were formed at a time when the area of the Weald was at a much higher level. The valleys in general are not wide but they provide some additional variety in the scenery.

Good Views

The views from the path are extensive for the most part, the scarp falling away directly to the pasture land and villages in the Gault clay and Greensand, the Greensand forming a secondary ridge where there is much heathland and natural conifer growth, as on the heights of Leith Hill. Beyond this stretches the clay of the High Weald itself with the edge of the South Downs visible in the further distance. On the downs the deciduous woodland is heavy and varied and in addition to beech, oak and ash there is much juniper, yew, whitebeam and box, while there are many kinds of grasses and the commoner, as well as some rare, wild flowers and butterflies.

The Pilgrims' Way

The North Downs Way was designed as a scenic walking route in its own right, and although the North Downs Way follows those parts of the traditional Pilgrims' Way where it has no hard surface and is not used by traffic, it often seeks a better, usually higher, line, so far as agricultural and other usage allows. It is this principle of a scenic route with good views which takes the North Downs Way straight along the downs to Folkestone and Dover.

The identification of the downland tracks with medieval pilgrims journeying from Winchester to Canterbury to visit the shrine of Saint Thomas à Becket, murdered at the instigation of Henry II in Canterbury in 1170, was not made until the eighteenth century and does not appear to be supported by any hard evidence. Pilgrims did go to Canterbury for this purpose, as Chaucer's Tales illustrate, and in the absence of roads as we know them and in view of the presumed wildness and danger of the lowlands, they could well have chosen a downland route. But most of the villages and their hostelries were, and are, situated well below the downs so that one must imagine the pilgrims coming down each night for their lodgings. In Kent at least the lower Watling Street would have been the more natural route though the Roman road could by this time have fallen into disrepair and become overgrown. These colourful associations, real or imagined, nevertheless add greatly to the interest of the route,

Man orchid

particularly as real doubt exists as to the facts. It is these doubts which are the basis for the extensive literature on the subject, of which the best known writing is Hilaire Belloc's *The Old Road*.

The Old Road

The extent of the path's connections with medieval pilgrimages may be doubted, but there is no question that a route on or close to the North Downs Way has been used for at least 2,000 years for trade and migration and to visit the religious centre at Stonehenge, in a similar manner to the South Downs Way and the Ridgeway Path. Since the North Downs route gives the most direct connection to the Continent, and since the Kent Coast has always been a convenient entry point for invaders, it was probably the most important of these routes at least until the building of Watling Street, and possibly later. Whatever may have been the case with pilgrims, primitive man would undoubtedly have preferred the mid-slopes of the downs, between the dangers of the ridge-top woods above and the equally great dangers and difficulties of what must have resembled a jungle below. In winter the slippery clay would have had no attraction for man or beast. Archaeological remains provide evidence of this usage though such evidence is less common than on the other two chalk highways; and the sunken lanes and terraced ways on the chalk themselves provide evidence of usage over a very considerable period indeed. This Hoar, or Old, Road continues beyond Farnham to Stonehenge and some say beyond to Cornwall for trading in tin, while the Pilgrims' Way must necessarily have taken a different course beyond Farnham to Winchester.

The route presents few difficulties and no hazards. The general direction along the downs is easily identified and where the Pilgrims' Way is followed the path can scarcely be mistaken, but elsewhere through fields and woods and where roads are joined or left or where there is more than one track the pattern is more intricate. A greater problem is that much of the approved route has not yet been established as a right of way and where reliable information is not available other rights of way, roads, or metalled parts of the Pilgrims' Way will have to be followed. In Kent the Pilgrims' Way is signposted as such, with the addition of a scallop shell (see left), associated in particular with St James of Compostella and the symbol of pilgrimage in general. This will mainly be by road where the traffic is relatively light.

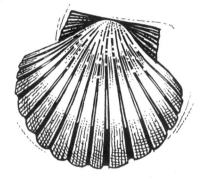

Scallop shell

Farnham to the Wey

The *North Downs Way* out of Farnham begins on the eastern outskirts of the town at the huge roundabout which connects the road from the town with the Farnham by-pass. A way through the roundabout and under the by-pass and railway leads up the Wey valley by Moor Park Lane to Moor Park. This house is now a college for further education, but it was here that Jonathan Swift met Stella, when he was secretary to Sir William Temple, diplomat and builder of the predecessor of the present Georgian house. A mile further up the valley between the river bank and a lake (past St Mary's Well, in a cave once inhabited by a benevolent witch called Mother Ludlam) are the ruins of Waverley Abbey, a Cistercian foundation of 1128.

From Moor Park Lane the approved route runs eastwards parallel to the A31, wending its way through the fields and plantations and round large residential properties to Seale and Puttenham. But the status of the route as right of way is uncertain and if no footpaths are available it will be best to proceed along the A31 and take the minor road at the foot of the Hog's Back past the huge clay pits, to Sandy Cross and Seale as far as the side road to the right leading to Puttenham Common, a distance of over three miles from Farnham; or some people may prefer simply to keep on this road into Puttenham. There are, however, no views from this road. For these you must climb up the Hog's Back, a thin strip of chalk sharply tilted into a ridge which is just wide enough to carry the busy A31, the North Downs at their slenderest. The views are away to the north towards the London basin, or southwards across the Wey valley, with in the foreground the tree-covered mass of Crooksbury Hill. The heathy area at Crooksbury is remarkable for its fine sandy soil, its pines and firs, its bridleways and the many fine houses hidden among the trees.

The eleventh-century church and priory at Puttenham would have had some significance for pilgrims, if such there were, for we are now on the Pilgrims' Way and will continue on it to well beyond Guildford. Our way leaves Puttenham by the path opposite the inn and leads over Puttenham Heath past the golf course, still on sandy soil, to the A3, where we pass conveniently under the road. We now cross the road which leads down to Compton village and join Sandy Lane. From here it is easy and pleasant going along a ridge with more conifers, but also some good views, past Loseley House and park on one hand and later Piccards Farm with views of the new Guildford Cathedral and University on the other, down to the Wey south of Guildford. Loseley is a very charming sixteenth-century house, open at certain times to the public, which was built with stones taken from Waverley Abbey at the dissolution. At the Guildford–Goldalming road, on a sandy height overlooking the river, are the remains of St Catherine's Chapel, the siting of which inevitably suggests that it was built there for the use of the pilgrims.

The lane leads down from the road to the river and towpath, and the site of a former ferry. The pilgrims are said to have crossed here. One can see the continuation footpath on the other bank by the different colour of the grass in the playing fields which it crosses. Plans have been made to carry the North Downs Way across the river by a well-designed new bridle-bridge near the ferry crossing point. There have been difficulties about the abutments of the bridge in the sandy, tree-clad slopes adjoining the river, about not interfering with passage along the towpath and concerning the privacy of adjoining cottages, but it is hoped that the bridge will be erected soon. Without it a detour along both banks is necessary to a footbridge nearly a mile upstream or down to the road crossing in Guildford.

Guildford to the Mole

East of the River Wey past the housing estate at Shalford we approach an extremely pleasant stretch of the North Downs Way, first along the north slopes of the wooded Chantries ridge and then straight across the road below Tyting Farm to St Martha's Church, placed squarely on its hill-top (see right). This beautifully sited isolated church, rebuilt in the mid-nineteenth century from a ruin, seems to epitomise the idea of the Pilgrims' Way and it is not hard to visualise medieval wayfarers on their way to Canterbury tarrying here. Hilaire Belloc thought that the yew

St Martha's Church

trees, which are much in evidence near the church and along the path, marked the line of the Pilgrims' Way, and since he attributed to them a very great age he believed their presence was a validation of the theory that the tracks along the downs were in fact used by pilgrims. But it is now thought that yew trees are common on the downs merely because the soil is suitable and that they are not in fact very old.

The path turns north along the Guildford–Albury road and then east to Newlands Corner. Here it is rare at any time not to see at least some visitors who have come in their cars to enjoy the extensive views southwards or to picnic in the cleared areas among the scrub-covered slopes of Albury Downs. The Surrey County Council have made a formal access agreement with the landowner which gives the public a right to be on the land and enables the council to warden the site, control the cars and generally to manage and improve the area in the interest of the visitors. The path is now firmly established along the main ridge of the North Downs on the way to the Mole valley and Dorking, at a general height of well over 600ft, overlooking the Tillingbourne valley, the A25, and the villages of Albury, Shere, Gomshall and Abinger Hammer. But the ridge is heavily wooded, planted predominantly with conifers, and the path along forestry rides and tracks gives few distant views. After Netley Heath, however, the path comes forward to the thinner growth of mixed deciduous woodland and bushes, with better views away to Leith Hill, on the shoulder of Hackhurst Downs and White Downs, and follows the hills round at uniform level to Ranmore Common, also a popular picnic site.

Looking east towards Dorking from the path on the White Downs

We cut straight across Ranmore road and down the roughly metalled road with wide verges that leads past Denbies, now largely demolished, and where the road turns sharply to the left we turn right towards Denbies Drive. The Mole valley opens out before us with Box Hill ahead and Dorking to one side. Norbury Park with its yew trees belongs to Surrey County Council and is open to the public, and Juniper Hill Field Centre is approached by the small road which joins the Mickleham by-pass (A24) at Burford Bridge. The break in the hills made by the Mole was used by the Romans to take Stane Street to London. The area has also literary and historic interest. Fanny Burney lived at Camilla Lacey (called after her novel, *Camilla*) on the west side of the valley; Keats and Robert Louis Stevenson stayed at what is now the Burford Bridge Hotel (as also did Lord Nelson); and George Meredith lived at Flint Cottage north of Box Hill. Juniper Hall (now the field studies centre) was once a shelter for refugees from the French Revolution and Talleyrand and Madame de Staël were put up there. The by-pass itself, a dual carriage with split levels, is well known as an early example of road landscaping and of the sensitive use of trees in reducing the impact of traffic on the countryside.

Box Hill to Oxted

There is a subway under the by-pass which comes up close to where a lane leads down to the river. This is crossed by stepping stones, and if these are covered there is a footbridge just downstream. We now begin the steep climb up Box Hill, thickly covered with whitebeams, yews and junipers,

North Downs Way on the Buckland Hills

as well as oak, beech and box. Closeness to London and easy road routes have made Box Hill a very popular place on fine summer days and the tramping of many feet has caused ugly scouring of the hillside. But although the visitors may detract from quiet contemplation of the natural beauty, Box Hill is still one of the best viewpoints on the route, overlooking the Mole valley, Dorking, the Weald and the line of the downs in both directions.

From Box Hill we resume our course along the upper edge of the downs to Betchworth Hills, above the great scars made by the chalk pits and lime-works, to Pebble Combe, where the path follows the line of the downs round the valley, and then along Buckland, Juniper and Colley Hills to Reigate Hill. This section, generally below the woods but also partly through woodland, provides some of the pleasantest views in Surrey, the prospect extending across the Weald ridge of Ashdown Forest as far, on a clear day, as the South Downs, where Chanctonbury Ring may be picked out, and along the downs themselves.

Behind these hills and not far from the path the M25 or South Orbital Motorway will run, dropping down at Merstham to the great multi-level interchange with the M23. We, however, cross Reigate Hill by the bridle-bridge across the road and continue down through Gatton Park to Merstham. The house at Gatton Park, first built in 1830, is now a school for orphans, and the park contains a tiny 'town hall', where before the 1832 Reform Bill two members of Parliament were elected; in 1542 Sir Roger Copley, the only inhabitant, elected both himself. Stone from Merstham quarries went into the building of the Palace of Westminster, the old London Bridge and Windsor Castle, and the first public railway ran from Merstham to London.

The way out of Merstham is by Shepherds' Hill above the large quarries, and thence by footpath and earth tracks past Hilltop Farm to White Hill and Gravelly Hill thence past Fosterdown Iron Age Fort to the A22 north of Godstone where we cross the road by a footbridge. We climb up near an old quarry site, pass a small industrial works and follow a broad track which takes us downhill to join a road and across to the viewpoint of Hanging Wood. We follow the slopes of Tandridge Wood below the woods, continuing at the same level through the National Trust property of South Hawk before curving round the lower edge of the immense Oxted chalk and cement works to meet the road climbing up the hill from Oxted and thence along the lower edge of Titsey Plantation. There are clear views outwards across the lowlands but at the foot of the hills is the fertile Vale of Holmesdale, in which lie the twin towns of Oxted and Limpsfield, and in the middle distance is the ridge of the Lower Greensand. A sunken lane takes us up from the plantation to Botley Hill, where the North Downs reach their highest point at 882ft, though the thick woods deny us the view outwards.

Titsey Park to the Medway

The path now goes through the woods above Titsey Park. Titsey Place is an eighteenth-century house with fine gardens and the large park contains the site of a Roman villa. When it was built the owner removed the church, which was inside the park, to its present site in the village. Shortly after passing Tatsfield church, and along a road with trees on the south side, the Surrey section of the path comes to an end and we enter Kent.

From the Biggin Hill road eastwards to Chevening Park the path follows the best course it can below the woods parallel to the road signposted as the Pilgrims' Way, at the foot of the hills. The last Earl of Stanhope, being without an heir, bequeathed the beautifully-sited mansion to the nation; it is to become the Prince of Wales's residence. We follow the contours skirting the northern edge of the park and descend to the road taking us over the by-pass to Dunton Green and on to Otford in the Darenth valley. This is a busy village which contains the remains of a palace of the Archbishop of Canterbury, and Lullingstone Roman villa down the valley may also be visited.

Up the nose of the downs again on the way to Wrotham the path takes the best course it can above the metalled Pilgrims' Way, making an irregular course through fields and woodland past Cotman's Ash to the point where the metalled road makes a sudden righthand bend. We descend quickly to take advantage of the unmetalled continuation of the Pilgrims' Way at the lower level, and follow it to the A20 at Wrotham. The views here are good. We have now, however, a difficult section of road and a large roundabout, and after that we have to start by taking the continuation of the metalled Pilgrims' Way again, but leave it for the lower edge of the woods leading to Trosley Towers. The village of Trottiscliffe (Trosley) lies below the downs separated by half a mile from its church and manor house at Court Lodge, whence it was moved at the time of the Black Death.

We now follow the gentle curve of the downs northwards where they have been cut by the Medway to make a wide valley, up to Holly Hill and Round Hill. The old tracks that we follow are tree-lined or through woodland of beech, hornbeam and yew. The views extend across the river to the distant horizon, across an intricate Kent landscape of woods, fields and orchards, with the villages of Offham, Addington, Ryarsh and West Malling in the foreground and the secondary ridge of the Lower Greensand behind them. A mile beyond Trosley Towers, before the path really begins to swing north, we pass above the megalithic tomb of the Coldrum, a burial chamber of unhewn stones, once covered with a mound. This Neolithic barrow and others in the area are matched by a similar monument on the other side of the valley, Kit's Coty, and by the Countless Stones, all formed from sarsen stones, or sandstone boulders, which were no doubt found scattered near the sites. Their siting has been adduced as evidence that early man did in fact make a detour some way down the Medway valley instead of venturing across the wide plain upstream, and that the crossing place was probably at Snodland. Our path would itself have crossed the river just slightly downstream, at Halling, if the ferry had still been in operation, but the Medway motorway bridge with its pedestrian crossing provided the opportunity of a suitable alternative without entering the urban area of Rochester.

The lower Medway valley itself, when seen from the downs on this side or on the other, is less than beautiful, with tall chimneys, electricity transmission lines, paper mills and cement works, but the immediate surroundings in either case are of great natural charm and peacefulness.

Rochester to the Stour

The downs on the east side of the river are Wouldham Downs and Burford Downs and there is a well-delineated track and lane to Bluebell

Hill, just above the prehistoric sites previously mentioned. The track leaves the scarp for a short time but returns to it along the woods above Boxley. There was a Norman abbey at Boxley which pilgrims would no doubt have visited but what remains is built into a private house. The busy A20 has to be negotiated into Detling after which we are back on the downs coming shortly to the overgrown remains, at Thurnham, of a Norman castle which may also have been a Roman settlement. The metalled Pilgrims' Way lies below and we remain above it as far as Hollingbourne, where again we come down to the lower level to follow the Pilgrims' Way as a rough track (though made up in places as an access to farms) the whole way into Charing, a distance of about seven miles.

The A20 (Watling Street) runs on the same course as the Way below the downs the whole way from Detling to Charing and frequently at no great distance from it, but the hurrying cars are lost in a view that reaches far across an ancient man-created landscape of woods, orchards, farms, hedges, hopfields, church towers, parkland and villages. At the foot of the hills is a string of villages—Thurnham, Hollingbourne, Harrietsham, Lenham—which would repay the time spent in a leisurely walk through their streets, on account of their medieval churches, old inns, manor houses and cottages of brick and timber.

Henry VIII, with a large retinue of lords and ladies, stayed at the palace of the Archbishop of Canterbury in Charing, now a farm, on his way to the Field of the Cloth of Gold in 1520, having no doubt made his way along the tracks followed by the long distance walker. The latter's interest today is likely to be directed to the old timber-framed houses of the village. We leave the village by the lane that runs above the very beautiful house of Petts Place and which carries lorry traffic from the quarries some way along it. The lane continues as an earth track among woodland almost to Dunn Street, a few houses overlooking the village of Westwell, where the author of *Ingoldsby Legends*, the Rev Richard Barham, was curate from 1814–1817. We arrive after a further mile at the ruins of Eastwell Church at the top end of a large artificial lake with water lilies. The church was a war casualty and from it has been removed the tomb of Richard Plantagenet, natural son of Richard III. Richard was a refugee from the Battle of Bosworth and spent his days unknown as a workman on the local estate. The nineteenth-century house at Eastwell Park is now demolished and the estate run as a farm.

The Stour to the Sea

Just after Boughton Lees the route to Canterbury and Dover branches off from the road, but we shall continue across the Stour valley to pick up the line of the downs and the main scenic route of the North Downs Way and follow it to Folkestone. We take a track south-eastwards through fields and orchards and across the old bridge over the river into the pleasant little town of Wye, where the University of London has an agricultural college and farm. This track continues on the other side of the town past St Eustace's Well, the waters of which are said to cure pilgrims' ailments, to Pickersdane Farm, where a footpath from the road leads us back up the downs. But from here the clear-cut character of the path as a ridge route tends to be spasmodic and we come down soon again to the road at Stowting, which lies in an embayment of the hills so that it is surrounded spaciously on three sides by the lowish hills. The chief interest is in the church which requires a short walk up the road from the route of the path.

From Stowting the scarp continues to be fragmented but the path keeps to the principle of following the high ground and avoiding the numerous small roads. Joseph Conrad lived in a farm near the hamlet of Postling and *Lord Jim* and *Typhoon* were written there. At Etchinghill the downs project forward and it is necessary to go to Brookman's Bushes at nearly 600ft for the better views. On the other side of Etchinghill we ascend an attractive coombe to join the final section of ridge which takes us into Folkestone. For most of the way the path runs close to a road which follows the contours and we walk just off it over Cherry Garden Hill, Castle Hill and Round Hill, where we look across Folkestone to the sea. Castle Hill is also called Caesar's Hill but the earthworks are not Roman but Iron Age with Norman additions. This brings us to the A260 which we cross and follow Creteway Down along the verges or just inside the fence of the A20 and the Valiant Sailor.

The path continues to Dover following the cliff edge above the Warren, where the chalk has slid over the underlying slippery clay and formed one of the great classical landslip areas of the country. The fallen debris in this vast area is covered with tree and scrub growth and is a favourite area for lovers of wild flowers. At the far end of the Warren we approach the Lydden Spout firing range and if the range is in use a detour has to be made up to the A20 at Abbotscliffe House and a return to the cliffs made at Hougham Lodge. It is then a clear and breezy walk over the turf of Shakespeare Cliff until Dover appears spread out below.

The Canterbury Loop

We must now return to the point overlooking the Stour valley, between

Chilham Square

Boughton Lees and Boughton Aluph, where the loop route to Canterbury makes its sudden turn north-east past Boughton Aluph's fourteenth-century church on its way up past Soakham Farm to Soakham Down and into the Great Forest of Challock where there is a clear track between the trees. Godmersham Park is on our right. Jane Austen was often a guest at the Georgian mansion which her brother Edward inherited, and *Mansfield Park* is said to be based on it. In Godmersham Church there is a medieval bas relief carving said to be of Becket. The path curves round the north side of Godmersham Park and makes a right-angled turn along a track following the eastern boundary of Chilham Park, which turns into a made-up path taking us down to the village of Chilham. Chilham Castle, the home of Viscount Massereene and Ferrard, is built on a hexagonal pattern and includes a Norman keep though the building is mainly Jacobean. The grounds were laid out by Capability Brown and contain a famous heronry. The village is largely unspoilt and attracts many visitors. The square (see page 121) is the main attraction, the castle entrance and the churchyard with its fourteenth-century church forming two sides and timbered Tudor and Jacobean buildings the other two sides.

Old Wives Lees, reached by road from Chilham, is modern. From here the way is mainly through orchards, colourful in spring, by Chartham Hatch and the earthworks of Bigberry Fort to the streets of a modern housing estate in Canterbury.

The path starts again on the east side of Canterbury leaving the A257 near the prison on a south-east course parallel to the A2 towards Dover. St Mary's Church at Patrixbourne is notable for the rich early medieval carvings round the doorway, and the village has some half-timbered houses. We continue over Barham Downs close to the A2 overlooking the Nail Bourne and with fine views to the north-west, and past the windmill into Womenswold. Barham Downs are remembered as the gathering place of armies; Roman legions and the armies of King John and of Simon de Montfort are said to have encamped here.

North-east of Shepherdswold are the Kent Colliery areas at Eythorne and Betteshanger. But from Coldred Court opposite an old earthwork the path takes a course through Waldershare Park where there are fine specimens of beeches, limes and chestnuts; it was recently proposed as a site for a wildlife park but refused permission. Scarcely out of the park, at Ashley, the path makes a sharp turn south to pick up the Roman road at Pineham. This highway ran between Dover and Richborough, where the Romans under Claudius landed in AD43. It is then a straight run, mostly over flattish land, into Dover.

10 · The Ridgeway Path

Opened: 29 September 1973
Length: 85 miles (136km)

A Downland Path of Great Antiquity

This path of 136km (85 miles) falls naturally into two distinct sections. One runs along the Chilterns escarpment south-westwards for 45 miles from Ivinghoe Beacon near Dunstable to the Thames at Goring. The other runs along the Great Ridgeway across the Berkshire Downs (now mostly in Oxfordshire) and merging into the Marlborough Downs in Wiltshire just south of Avebury. The dividing line at the Goring Gap is where the Thames breaks through what is geologically one great chalk band stretching from Salisbury Plain to the Wash. It is possible that at some future date the path will be extended along this band, southwards and westwards round Salisbury Plain, still following the historic course of the great Ridgeway, and over Cranborne Chase in Dorset to Seaton on the Devon coast, thus linking with the South-West Peninsula Coast Path. In the other direction an extension past Dunstable and Luton would take in the outlying chalk hills in the Hitchin area, but an extension beyond this to the coast, although it would link with the proposed Peddar's Way and the Norfolk Coast Path, is less likely because the chalk in this area is a much less distinctive landscape feature.

While the path along the Chilterns is continuous as a footpath only, the rest of the route is a bridleway throughout its 45 miles and as such is open to cyclists as well as horse-riders. Not all of the Chilterns paths are yet rights of way and care must be taken not to trespass.

The land which the path crosses shows the distinctive smooth landforms of chalk country with short grass on thin soil, large fields and sweeping hill-sides, dry valleys and delicate colouring, particularly when it is ploughed. There are almost no houses on the hills, which gives a deceptive feeling of isolation, and there is a lot of evidence of early human usage and settlement. In these respects it has much in common with the North and South Downs Ways, and this is not surprising since all three areas are part of the same geological system.

The Chilterns

The Chilterns section of the path overlooks and gives magnificent views

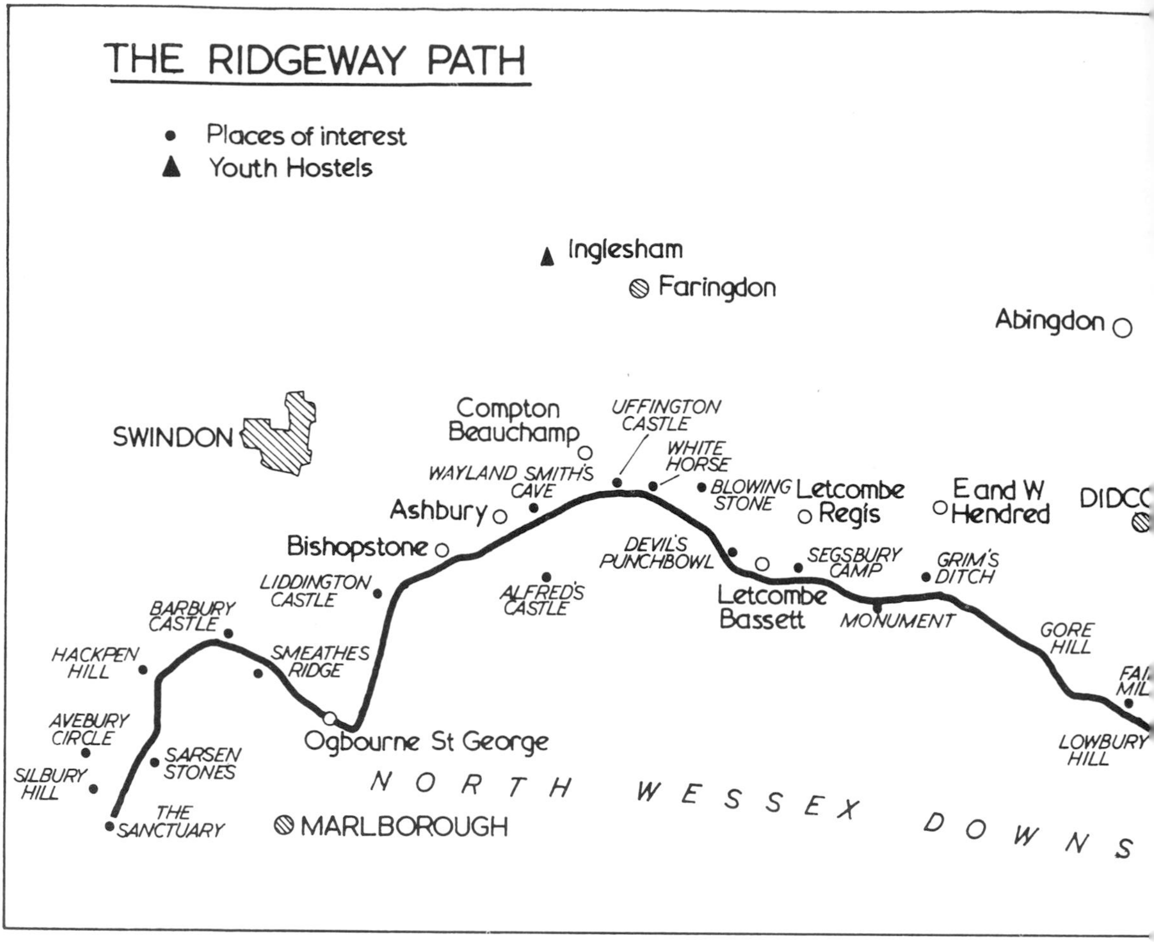

THE RIDGEWAY PATH

- • Places of interest
- ▲ Youth Hostels

▲ Inglesham

◎ Faringdon

Abingdon ○

SWINDON

Compton
Beauchamp ○

UFFINGTON
CASTLE

WHITE
HORSE

WAYLAND SMITH'S
CAVE

• BLOWING
STONE

Letcombe ○
○ Regis

E and W
○ Hendred

DIDCC
◎

Ashbury ○

Bishopstone ○

DEVIL'S
PUNCHBOWL

○

SEGSBURY
CAMP

GRIM'S
• DITCH

LIDDINGTON
CASTLE

ALFRED'S
CASTLE

Letcombe
Bassett

MONUMENT

GORE
HILL

BARBURY
CASTLE

SMEATHES
RIDGE

FAI
MIL

HACKPEN
HILL

AVEBURY
CIRCLE

SARSEN
STONES

Ogbourne St George

N O R T H   W E S S E X   D O W N S

LOWBURY
HILL

SILBURY
HILL

THE
• SANCTUARY

◎ MARLBOROUGH

across the Aylesbury plain, making its winding way from hill-top to hill-top, where the great fingers of chalk headland, here frequently overlain with 'clay with flints', stretch outwards over the clay lowlands. Great beech woods cover about a fifth of the whole downland area, including parts of the escarpment, so that in places the path is forced downwards to maintain the views. The path also goes through the woods, some of the most splendid woods in England. The trees are best seen in early May when the buds burst into a light green and the woodland floor is a colourful pattern of bluebells and primroses, or in October when the brittle leaves turn to bright browns and yellows; later, in November, the ground is a carpet of red and gold.

Celtic tribes, Romans, Saxons, Danes and Normans have lived in, and fought over, the Chilterns area and have left their marks. William the Conqueror came this way in his approach to London. It is the country of John Hampden and of Chequers. Among the historic survivals along the path is Grim's Ditch, a lengthy section of which is followed where the path approaches the Thames and which is close to the path elsewhere. This

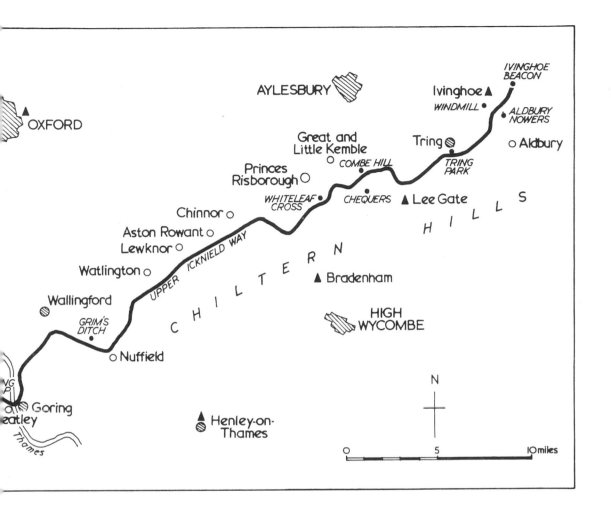

earthwork has been ploughed up in many places, but in others reaches a
height of more than 6ft from the top of the dyke to the bottom of the
ditch. It appears to be Saxon or Danish but its purpose is not clear. It is
unlikely as a defence work but may have been a tribal boundary or even
the boundary line between Mercia and Wessex, thus serving much the
same purpose as Offa's Dyke. A long section of the Upper Icknield Way is
also included in the Chilterns Path (the Lower Icknield Way is now
metalled road) at its western end. Named after the Iceni tribe, it is
probably pre-Roman and arose in the same way as the historic tracks
along the North and South Downs and the Ridgeway, of which it will
have been a part, all routes leading to Avebury and Stonehenge, from
where other routes would have taken travellers to points further west.
Like the North Downs route, and unlike the other two, the Upper
Icknield Way follows a course part-way up the scarp slope and not its top,
a choice which was no doubt suggested by the topographical and climatic
conditions of the time and one in which the thick woodlands above, then
as now, may well have played an important part. It is nonetheless high

Walkers approaching Ivinghoe
Beacon from the west

enough, where it is used, to command clear views over the immediate countryside adjoining it.

At each of several gaps in the downland wall there are small but lively towns—Tring, Wendover, Princes Risborough—each gap also being used to thread a main road and railway through the hills on their way northward or westward from London. In the case of the Tring gap there is also the Grand Union Canal and the River Bulbourne, the other two gaps being dry. West of Princes Risborough the hill front is unbroken and we have in its shelter a chain of quiet unassuming villages and small towns—Chinnor, Aston Rowant, Lewknor, Watlington, Britwell and Ewelme.

The Great Ridgeway

The Ridgeway west of the Thames follows a majestic and sinuous course along the almost unbroken escarpment above the Vale of the White Horse. The landscape is much more open for although there are trees in the sheltered valleys and occasional spinneys and clumps on the edge itself the downs are not heavily wooded, and the general impression is of bareness. This feeling increases as one goes westward. The grass or earth track is 30ft wide in places, and often it runs at some distance from the edge so that one has to come off the path to a headland for views over the plain. Sometimes it runs between hedges, at others it narrows between brambles and bushes or runs over open downland. In wet weather the surface may be churned up and muddy from the passage of tractors, for the long established status of the Ridgeway as a byeway over which there is a right to take vehicles is jealously guarded, and in dry weather this results in deep, hard ruts which also make hard going for walker or rider. It is unimpeded by gates along its entire 40 miles. The occasional car may be encountered along the Ridgeway, but most motorists are deterred by the poor surface and cars will most often be found parked at a short distance from the nearest road, while the occupants picnic alongside or walk a short way along the path. But motor-cyclists are less deterred by the poor conditions, and apart from single riders or groups the track is occasionally used for trials and scrambles.

Ancient Peoples

The origins of the Ridgeway track are lost in the mists of time. It seems likely that it already existed when the great religious monuments of unhewn stone were set up at Avebury to serve some unknown cult (2000BC, and older than Stonehenge). In a heavily forested country it is likely that the 'chalkways' were the only possible highways, and Avebury and Stonehenge were at the meeting place of many routes. The light soils of the chalk proved capable of being worked by primitive implements and there was an abundance of flints for the making of axes and other tools, so that settlement was encouraged. The barrows constructed by these and later peoples for burials are extremely numerous along the path and in the surrounding area. Considerable organisation, effort and skill must have been required in their construction. Many more have been ploughed up, particularly in recent years as a result of large-scale farming methods.

Later peoples followed the Ridgeway as settlers or as traders bringing gold and gold ornaments from Ireland and Wales and tin from Cornwall, and carrying pottery and other manufactured goods or luxuries in the other direction from Europe and the East. It is these peoples who have left the most remarkable monuments on the Ridgeway apart from Avebury, namely, the hill-forts or 'castles' at Liddington, Barbury, Uffington and Segsbury. Whether these massive circular earth ramparts were defended settlements of Iron Age peoples, or staging posts along the route (they are roughly at intervals of twenty miles) it is not possible to say. Today they are objects for speculation and wonder. The interest they and the many other ancient and mysterious works along the route arouse—burial chambers, round and long barrows, Celtic fields and lynchets, standing stones and circles, the huge mound at Silbury Hill, Wayland's Smithy, Wansdyke, the White Horse at Uffington—transcends for some people even the great beauty of the landscape.

There are no settlements along the Ridgeway Path but at the spring-line below the downs where chalk and clay meet and water is available, there is again a series of villages and hamlets—East and West Hendred, Letcombe Regis and Letcombe Bassett, Compton Beauchamp, Ashbury, Bishopstone and Liddington among others. These are of interest for their churches, manor houses and brick and flint or thatched buildings, but for accommodation it may be necessary to descend to Wantage, a little further to Marlborough, or even to Swindon. The downs are not, as yet, a tourist area on a grand scale.

The Route: Ivinghoe Beacon to Princes Risborough

The Ridgeway Path begins at the top of Ivinghoe Beacon (see opposite).

just off the B489 road roughly halfway between Dunstable and Tring and within the National Trust property of Ashridge Forest. The path, scoured in the chalk, descends from the Beacon across the minor road coming up the downland scarp and follows tracks southwards through scrub to Steps Hill and round the top of the deeply incised dry valley of Incombe Hole to Pitstone Hill. Among the hedgerows and farmland below, the windmill at Ivinghoe may be picked out on the right. Soon we are standing above the tall chimneys and buildings of the huge Pitstone cement works, but these offend less from above than below, where the hillside scars are visible.

Aldbury Nowers, which follows, is a wooded retreat with secluded dells among tall trees where the ground is hazed with bluebells in the spring and the paths lined with cowslip and violets. The gem village of Aldbury, complete with village green and pond, stocks, an ancient church and pretty timber-clad houses, lies just to the east and within easy reach.

The Tring gap with its roadworks and railway has to be crossed, but the walker will be tempted to pause and observe the canal. We do not enter Tring but skirt the woodland of Pendley Manor, now a centre for adult education, and enter the woods of Tring Park, formerly the home of the Rothschild family but now owned by Tring Council. There are some very fine specimen trees. There is more woodland as we continue along the edge past Hastoe village, cutting off the huge promontory mass of forest (Wendover Forest Park) that overlooks Wendover and the services camp area at Halton, before we come to open land again at Cock's Hill. We

View from Coombe Hill near Wendover

have passed unobserved our first long but discontinuous section of Grim's Ditch to the south with Cholesbury Camp a little further away.

There is a further gap in the hills at Wendover. These gaps may have been cut by north–south flowing rivers, long disappeared in this case, when the clay vale to the north was at a much higher level than at present. Wendover has some interesting timbered buildings and old inns, in one of which, the Red Lion, Oliver Cromwell stayed in 1642. The manor house once belonged to John Hampden, and there are sixteenth-century wall paintings in Bosworth House.

We continue on a line now directly overlooking the plain of Aylesbury, climbing through beechwoods to Bacombe Hill, less than a mile above Wellwick Farm, the home of Judge Jeffreys, and on to the top of Coombe Hill, the highest point on the route, where at 850ft there are exceptional views in all directions (see opposite). The monument on the top is in memory of the dead in the Boer War. We descend from the open top of Lodge Hill by road and turn southwards along the lower edge of Longwalk Wood, thus omitting from the walk the high point of Beacon Hill, where is Cymbeline's Castle overlooking the Kimbles. Our path takes us to the road in front of Chequers Park, the thirteenth-century manor house which is the country home of the Prime Minister. The route previously followed a right of way through the park but the path was closed in 1972, for security reasons, and we now continue westward again to the scarp south of Pulpit Hill where there is an Iron Age encampment.

Princes Risborough to the Thames

On the face of Whiteleaf Hill, above the timber and thatch cottages of Monks Risborough, a large white cross is cut into the chalk hillside, and there are more good views. The path then descends to the Upper Icknield Way and the southern outskirts of Princes Risborough (named after the Black Prince) where the old Market House in the centre of the town, crowned by a turret and clock, is of interest. We take the main road south out of the town through a further gap in the hills, and take the first road to the right which leads to a footpath across the railway and up to the downs again and across the grassy knoll of another Lodge Hill. This path, which overlooks Princes Risborough, continues straight to meet the Icknield Way at Hempton Wainhill.

The path from Wendover has been mainly along the scarp, along hedges or across fields or alongside or through woods, taking an irregular course with fairly frequent changes in direction, up and down slopes and over stiles and through gates, along lanes, over narrow earth or grass tracks or through woodland rides. The view has been of distant fields or near at hand of verdant valleys, well cared-for woods and snug farmhouses. At Hempton Wainhill we turn round the northern edge of the magnificent Bledlow Great Wood (where another cross is cut in the hillside) and join the Upper Icknield Way. Here the path takes on a different character. For seven miles it now runs without interruption almost in a straight line along the foothills as a broad track between hedges and fences. Above on the left are the steepest slopes of the whole Chilterns range, covered by some of its finest beechwoods, and below runs the disused track of the railway that formerly connected Watlington with Chinnor. At the start of this section is the second large cement works on our route, at Chinnor.

The Icknield Way has been close at hand all the way from the start of the route near Ivinghoe Beacon, for it starts in East Anglia and continues to Avebury. But as low-level, surfaced roads neither of the two versions, upper or lower, has had much practical interest for us. Perhaps the lower highway was made by the Romans after all, or perhaps they adopted one of the two or more highways which already existed. At any rate it has been said that edible Roman snails may still be found along the route. Only a stone's throw from the route a string of villages press upon each other along the Lower Icknield Way—after Chinnor come Aston Rowant, Lewknor, Watlington, Britwell, Ewelme. All have something of old-fashioned charm to offer, but Ewelme, only slightly further away than the others, is the epitome of an English village.

The path climbs up the hills again from the Icknield Way by the side of Britwell Hill and continues southwards by Swyncombe and Ewelme Park to the busy A423. Through the entrance to the Huntercombe Golf Course we emerge on to Nuffield Common and are soon in Nuffield village. All this has been deep, rolling countryside but the Chilterns have now come almost to their end and already we are looking forward to the downs across the River Thames. But there is one last long section which takes us along the low line of Grim's Ditch itself for nearly three miles to Mongewell Park and thence down at a short distance from the river bank to North Stoke and along the towpath to South Stoke. Here the towpath switches banks and we should have crossed and followed it if the ferry to Moulsford had not long since ceased to function. So we continue by a bridle track to Goring and cross to Streatley by the road bridge instead. This interlude along the river makes a pleasant change from the hills we have followed and those to come.

Goring Gap to Uffington Castle

The narrow gorge of the Goring Gap is of geological interest and several theories have been advanced to explain why the Thames cuts through the chalk instead of continuing to meander in the Oxford Clay Vale. Either the clay was level with or higher than the chalk when the valley was cut in the normal way, and an enormous amount of erosion has taken place; or melt-water trapped behind the hills and in front of glaciers in the Ice Age scoured the gap as it burst out through the chalk to escape southwards. The other Chilterns gaps would have been formed in the same way.

We turn north along the main road at Streatley and keeping left at the fork take the first lane on the left which goes past some houses and becomes a rough track again at Warren Farm. From Thurle Down there are long views back to the Chilterns across the Thames. Soon we meet a cross track leading, on the right, to the site of a Roman temple and a small Iron Age encampment on Lowbury Hill, though there is little to see on the ground, and if one followed it further to a fragment of Grim's Ditch and, further still, to the hill-fort on the outlier of Blewburton Hill. This Iron Age camp looks down on the village of Aston Tirrold, the first of many pretty villages strewn along at the foot of the hills. But we pass over the crossroads to join the continuation of the Fair Mile coming up the valley. We could have chosen this approach to the downs by continuing further along the road out of Streatley instead of coming up past the golf course by Thurlestone Down. The Fair Mile is a very broad track indeed

but on a summer's day it is likely to be lined with parked cars and apart from the longer walk along the busy road this is what we want to avoid.

Across the disused Didcot–Newbury railway-line we turn right at an approach road to Compton Agricultural Research Station and start our long march along the edge of the downs escarpment with open views again across the northern plain. Over Several Down and Sheep Down we come to Gore Hill where the A34 sweeps down the hill (there will certainly be cars and lorries parked among the scattered trees at the crossing) followed by more downland to Scutchamer Knob and the tumulus beside the track. Here the downs nudge forward above the low bank of Grim's Ditch as it follows the hills' contours. In the middle distance are more pretty villages—East and West Hendred, the Lockinges and Ardington—but further away still we see the huge cooling towers of Didcot Power Station and also the Harwell Atomic Energy Station. At Ridgeway Down overlooking Wantage the monument is to Lord Wantage, the town being just two and a half miles down the road.

Less than a mile past this road the path takes a sharp left turn but quickly resumes its general direction past Whitehouse Farm and across the Wantage road (A338) where we come to the first of the hill-forts on the route at Segsbury Castle (or Letcombe) overlooking the secluded villages of Letcombe Regis and Letcombe Bassett with their pleasant streams and watercress beds. The camp is a great circular compound enclosing twenty-seven acres cut in two by the road down to Letcombe Regis, no doubt through the original entrances. In spite of the effects of time and weather the ramparts are impressive. Within them the men and women who tended the surrounding fields would have crowded in times of danger,

Riders on the Ridgeway Path to the south of Wantage, looking westwards towards Letcombe Bassett (*A F Kersting*)

View of Hackpen Hill

together with cattle, sheep, pigs, goats and horses. The wall tops would have been protected by stakes and the walls would have had a cladding of stones with a ditch around them. The entrances would have been narrow with wooden gates and further protective earthworks; and inside there were no doubt clusters of wood and thatch huts. The camp would in effect have been a walled village, of the same kind but on a smaller scale as Maiden Castle.

Next comes into view the Devil's Punchbowl, a great steep-sided coombe in the hillside almost isolating Hackpen Hill from the downland ridge. The Seven Barrows are a mile away on the other side of the path and for those interested a road leads almost to them. Racehorses will most likely be seen in this area for this is horse-training country and Lambourn is not far away. The Blowing Stone may be seen, and blown, in the garden of a house at the bottom of the road to Kingston Lisle just a little further on. The story is that King Alfred summoned his troops with it, for this is Alfred country and his statue has pride of place in Wantage town square.

Uffington to Avebury

We are now approaching White Horse Hill and on fine weekends throughout the year and at bank holidays you are unlikely to be alone there for cars and coaches crawl painfully up from below to disgorge scores of sightseers at the large car-park at the top. The great earth walls of Uffington Castle are climbed joyfully by the children while the more inquisitive of the parents will gaze at them in puzzlement, if they are not

The ramparts of Uffington Castle (*A F Kersting*)

more taken up by the view, which is far-reaching and magnificent. Below the hill is the great sweep of the Manger, with the famous White Horse carved in the chalk above it. Dragon's Hill, where St George slew the dragon, is also below. Down to the left is Hardwell Camp where King Ethelred is said to have encamped before the Battle of Ashdown, with the moated manor of Compton House across the road in Compton Beauchamp village.

A mile further on is Wayland's Smithy, a chambered Neolithic tomb where the inner stone structure of the long barrow has been laid bare and opened to the public. Eight skeletons were found when the site was excavated. The symbol of the horse, which has become attached to this burial place, is important in Scandinavian mythology. The story is that Wayland the Smith lived in a cave on the site (ie within the chambered barrow) and re-shod overnight the horses of those who left money in payment, but never himself appeared. Iron bars, thought to be money tokens, were in fact found during the excavations in 1919. Some say that the White Horse at Uffington was cut by King Alfred to celebrate his victory over the Danes. Scientific archaeology gives no clue to its date or to the reason why it is there. Alfred's name has also been attached to Alfred's Castle, another Iron Age fort a mile to the south, and the area abounds in similar antiquities and in legends of King Arthur's and earlier times. This area was also the background to Thomas Hughes' novel *Tom Brown's Schooldays*.

The track continues to Fox Hill, with more villages just below—Ashbury, Bishopstone, Little Hinton, Liddington—across the M4, and we turn off the A419 to Liddington Castle lying in the grazing land just below the path. As large as Segsbury and equally impressive, there is, however, no footpath leading to the earthworks. The historic Ridgeway proceeds in a straight line from the A419 below Liddington Castle across the lower ground south of Chiseldon and ascends the hills again at Barbury Castle. We do not take this course but turn south along the hills overlooking the valley of the River Og along a track which prefers to run straight rather than follow the sinuous course of the scarp edge (which is here crowded with old earthworks) to a point where we can turn sharply right across the old railway line to Marlborough and into Ogbourne St George.

Up westwards again above the military camp we soon join Smeathe's Ridge, one of the most delightful tracks on the route with beautiful views on either side, and soon reach Barbury Castle, where we pass right through the earthworks. This camp occupies a commanding site with good views all round, Swindon lying immediately to the north. Within the twelve acres of enclosed ground many implements, coins and items of decoration have been found. Our track then takes us curving round the steep scarp southwards past Hackpen Hill and more views. On Fyfield and Overton Downs there are vast expanses of sarsen stones, also called grey wethers because of their resemblance to sheep. These stones are the remains of a layer of rock which once covered the chalk but is now weathered away; they have been a useful source of building material in the area and were used in the monuments at Avebury and Stonehenge.

Avebury

Avebury is an older centre of pilgrimage than Stonehenge and no walker

Avebury Ring

of the Ridgeway should fail to spend some time there. An earth bank and ditch, even today some 15ft high, encloses a large area in which a circle of unhewn sarsen stones (see left), some of huge dimensions, were set up. Originally one hundred in number but now much depleted they possibly represent alternately men and women, larger stones being erected at the entrances. Two further stone circles lie inside the outer circle, originally each of thirty stones, but only a few of these have survived. Some of the missing stones are built into the church and other buildings in the village, the villagers having found an ingenious way of breaking the stones by piling brushwood around them, setting it alight and then throwing cold water over them. A busy road goes straight through the enclosed area and another one cuts it transversely, using in both cases the original entrances. Avebury also has a beautiful Elizabethan manor house, an old church, ancient barns and some other old houses, and a museum where finds made in the area can be seen.

Leading from the stone circle to West Kennett is the mile-long Kennett Avenue, the remains of a processional way consisting of two lines of stones ending at the Sanctuary just south of the Bath road. Our route passes close to it. The remarkable ritual monuments at Avebury are shrouded in mystery. What ceremonies were performed there are a matter for the individual imagination and are likely to remain so, the only clues provided being those of the stones themselves.

There are other archaeological puzzles nearby within easy reach of the path. Silbury Hill is a mile to the west along the Bath road, a 130ft mound round which runs the Roman road, showing that the mound was there first. It may have been a huge tumulus, the burial place of an important

The Ridgeway Path going south
from Avebury

dynasty, but no one really knows its purpose or when or why it was built. Excavations made most recently in the 1960s have yielded nothing of real interest. The Long Barrow at West Kennett which dates from about 2500BC is remarkable for its size, being 350ft long and 80ft wide at its widest, and contains several burial chambers where large numbers of skeletons have been found. The supporting and covering stones have been exposed for inspection. Windmill Hill, north-west of Avebury, consists of three concentric earthworks dating from about 2500BC whose purpose is equally mysterious. Round and long barrows, Roman roads, and earthworks of British, Saxon and Danish origin are to be found all over the area.

The path meets the Bath road at a café, crosses over the road by the Sanctuary and ends, for the moment, at West Kennett village.

11 · More Long Distance Paths?

A number of new long distance paths have been suggested from time to time but whether any of them will be adopted remains to be seen. A brief description follows of some of the proposed paths.

A New Bridle Route

The *Dartmoor Way* would run northwards from Plymouth into the Dartmoor National Park, turning eastwards across the great wilderness of granite moorland in the direction of Ashburton. North of the Tavistock–Ashburton road (A384), one of only two main roads that cross the moor, it will make a great loop round the whole northern part of the national park, ending at South Zeal. As a long distance bridleway it would be open to horse-riders as well as walkers. At one time it was projected that the bridleway route would continue northwards from South Zeal through the rich agricultural land which lies between Dartmoor and Exmoor and go on across the Exmoor National Park, to meet the sea at Lynton in the west and at Minehead in the east. This concept was based on the idea of an old Mariners' Way which allegedly linked the North and South Devon ports. This larger scheme (The Two Moors Way) has not been proceeded with because of lack of agreement on the suitability of the land between the two national parks for a long distance bridleway. Local agricultural interests reacted unfavourably to the proposal, believing that recreational facilities should be concentrated within the boundaries of the national parks and that the terrain was not in any case suitable for horse-riding.

The route will cross some very lonely and uncompromising areas. The landscape consists of great tracts of inhospitable, boulder-strewn country with heather moor and coarse grasses, high granite tors and smooth and windswept hills rising gently one behind the other, interspersed with bog. It is also a country of rushing rock-strewn streams, and colourful with mosses and lichens which cover every bare surface. There was no glaciation in the area and there are no lakes, but with the high rainfall and impervious rock, water seems to dominate the scene, in the movement of

Typical Dartmoor saddle tor

the fast-flowing streams, the bogs, the mosses and the mists for which Dartmoor is famous. Although sheep and wild ponies wander freely, the hard, unyielding granite and the acid soil have almost wholly resisted agricultural exploitation, so that the landscape presents much the same appearance as it must have done to Neolithic and Bronze Age man, whose works are scattered profusely along the path. The metamorphic and sedimentary rocks bordering the high moor, however, have been less resistant to geological change and the path also passes through deep gorges where the rivers have cut deeply and whose shelter has encouraged the growth of a thick mantle of natural woodland.

Standing stones, hut circles, prehistoric cairns and Bronze Age villages add much of interest to the natural scene and are in many places the only works of man that can be seen. In medieval times Dartmoor Forest was a royal hunting reserve but following the discovery of tin a number of small towns such as Tavistock, Okehampton and Ashburton, now known as stannary towns, began to flourish. Until the late Middle Ages Dartmoor rivalled Cornwall as a tin-producing area but the deposits were quickly worked out, though some activity continued until before World War I. Examples of the blowing stones, hollowed rocks in which the tin was smelted, may still be found on the moors. In recent times the enclosure of open moor by 'new takes' has proceeded, and as in Cornwall the granite has also led to the exploitation of china clay deposits, large devastated areas occurring in the area north-west of Plymouth. Rights of common over the moor are enjoyed collectively by residents of the nearby towns and villages, and the ponies which graze together on the moors are owned by commoners whose animals are individually marked.

The path is linked to the South-West Peninsula route at Turnchapel across the water from Plymouth but a person starting the route from the south is more likely to begin from the A38 at Plympton, where a path leads up alongside the old railway track to Yelverton up the valley of the Plym River and into thick woodland along the valley side. At Shaugh Prior close to the extensive china clay workings we enter the national park, keeping close to the river as far as Cadover Bridge, a popular spot for family picnics in the summer. Across the valley we keep ascending by the river, the now bare hill-sides towering up on either side, the tops crowned with granite tors and rock clitters. This lonely area is remarkable for the very large number of hut circles, enclosures and cairns that crowd the valley.

At the headwaters of the river we join the Abbot's Way, and cross a spongy area of blanket bog to the headwaters of the Erme and then the Avon. We are soon descending Scorriton Down to the roads on the eastern edge of the national park to Holne village. Across the River Dart by Holne Bridge on the main road we climb towards the moor again through the lovely woods of the valley of the Dart, continuing by the Webburn to Ponsworthy and along the moor edge above Widecombe and up to Hamel Down and Hameldown Tor, beside which is Grimspound, one of the best-known of the prehistoric religious monuments on the moor.

Across the Moretonhampstead road to Chagford Common we pass Fernworthy Reservoir and more stone monuments to the Walla Brook and Scorhill Circle. Religious monuments are so plentiful on the moor that it must have had some special significance similar to the areas near

Avebury and Stonehenge. By Throwleigh Common and South Tawton Common, where a path leads down to South Zeal, we come to Belstone village where we take the moor path that leads to Okehampton Military Camp. Military roads lead southwards here deep into the moor to the area where live firing takes place. The path gradually turns again to complete its circle past the new Meldon Dam to Sourton Down and on round the hill-edges past Lydford to the military training area at Willsworthy.

We now turn again across the Tavy River and across the open moor to join the Lich Way, taking us to Wistman's Wood, a residual area of ancient natural woodland of great interest, where the twisted and stunted tree trunks are encrusted with mosses and lichens. We cross the Moretonhampstead road again near Powder Mill Cottages, leaving it through the Forestry Commission plantation for Bellever and straight on to join the route we have followed on the eastern side of the moor.

A Roman Road and Along the Coast

The *East Anglian Way* is made up of two parts which are very different in character. The Peddar's Way, a Roman road, leads straight and purposefully northwards from near Thetford in Norfolk to the Wash. It runs for about forty-one miles through generally flat country, which includes heath and breckland with sandy soil and many new plantations, as well as good East Anglian agricultural land. At Hunstanton it turns along the coast where it runs along low cliffs and dunes and along the edge of saltings and marshland and through a number of holiday towns, also taking in or going near some old and attractive villages. It could well continue further southwards along this coast in Suffolk.

The Peddar's Way probably continued southwards to Colchester, and at the Wash there could well have been a ferry linking it with a route to the Roman settlement at Lincoln, thus saving a detour round the impassable and perhaps dangerous fenland. The Icknield Way also ends at the Wash and runs close to Grime's Graves, primitive man's major source of flint tools in southern England; and just as the Romans appear to have adopted one of the two tracks of the Icknield Way, they may also have adopted the Peddar's Way. It has been lost in places and is in part a surfaced road but otherwise has the appearance of a green lane, running between trees or with hedges and fields on either hand. There is an almost complete absence of houses or other buildings actually on the route. The open skies, and the knowledge that this trackway has survived unchanged through so many centuries (it was used until recently as a drove road) make up in some measure for the flatness of the track and the surrounding country. It is suitable for use as a bridleway, and unlike the South Downs Way or the Ridgeway Path its flatness is a positive advantage for cyclists.

The long views across the landscape from the coast path, the lonely emptiness of the saltings where the water creeps along innumerable creeks, the atmospheric haze which blurs objects at a distance but which is punctuated by the strong colour of sails or the sharp outline of a fowler's hut, and the vast open skies, give it a character which is not present on any other route. There is much very ordinary development in the towns and one is never far from people, traffic and houses, but there are also old houses of brick and wood or brick and flint, and flint churches; and there is especially the wildlife of the coast. Because of the vast numbers of birds of many kinds which breed among these secluded salt marshes and dunes or visit them during migration, the area is probably the richest in the country for bird-watching and the scientific observation of bird habits and behaviour.

Three miles east of Thetford the Peddar's Way, coming up from the River Ouse, crosses the A1066 and then the River Thet near the site of a Roman villa, and marches straight through or alongside plantations over heathland to East Wretham. There is a services area north of the village and the path we take is not the historic line of the Peddar's Way, but to the east of it either by the track of a disused railway line or by road through the hamlet of Thompson, where there is a large barrow, lending support to the idea that the Peddar's Way was pre-Roman. A short way beyond is Merton Park and we pass the church and the churchyard where Edward FitzGerald, translator of the *Rubáiyát of Omar Khayyám*, is buried. At Little Cressingham is another barrow. Still in the sandy area of the Breckland we pass between South and North Pickenham and then east of Swaffham where the legend of the pedlar is remembered. The pedlar (or peddar) journeyed from Swaffham (no doubt along the Peddar's Way) to London in search of riches only to meet another pedlar journeying north who told him he was going to Swaffham also in search of riches. So the pedlar returned home and there in due course he found his riches.

Castle Acre Priory

Castle Acre is a breckland village of flint houses and narrow streets, and has a great deal of character as well as historic interest. There is a great archway through which one goes into the main street. The ruins of the priory (see above) lie romantically situated in meadows by the River Nar and consist of a great façade of intricate workmanship in stone, and other wall fragments. There are also the ruins of a Norman castle and a Roman site.

The Peddar's Way out of Castle Acre is a road which runs dead straight to Great and Little Massingham, after which we touch the edge of Houghton Park, which was built for Sir Robert Walpole in 1721 and has fine carvings. King's Avenue runs to the left at Anmer to Sandringham Park where the grounds are open to the public when the royal family is not in residence. The Peddar's Way then runs straight for the next six miles to the sea.

For its first fifteen miles from Holme-next-the-Sea the coast path would make its way as best it can, avoiding marshy saltings sometimes drained by water channels and numerous reedy creeks. A large area at Scolt Head Island belongs to the National Trust and the island may be visited by boat to see the terns, gannets, skuas and oyster-catchers as well as many varieties of ducks and geese. Horatio Nelson was born in 1758 in a parsonage (now demolished) at Burnham Thorpe just slightly inland. Salt marshes again stretch for five miles from Wells-next-the-Sea to another National Trust area of marshy flats at Blakeney, similar to Scolt and of interest for the variety and rarity of its wild flowers. There is an eighteenth-century windmill at Cley-next-the-Sea. The path would then continue along a firmer coastline of shallow cliffs to Sheringham, Cromer and Mundesley and to Bacton where the terminal installations for North Sea Gas are located. There follows a long length of straight unbroken cliff backed by agricultural land and much scattered development to Caister and Great Yarmouth.

More Downland

The *Wolds Way* is a continuation of the Cleveland Way, running from Filey back along the northern well-defined escarpment of the Yorkshire Wolds almost to Malton, and then generally south where the westward-facing scarp is much less well defined, to end on the Humber estuary six miles west of Kingston upon Hull. This is also chalk country but the chalk is harder and the hills do not show smoothly flowing contours to the same extent as, for example, the South Downs. The ridge line of the downs is also more broken particularly where it runs north–south, due to the action of Ice Age rivers which scoured valleys that are now dry. These form pleasant dales of which advantage is taken by the route. Like the other chalk areas the wolds were previously associated with sheep-rearing but are now mostly richly cultivated farmland, the cultivation extending in some places right over the scarp as well as the dip slopes. This creates difficulties for the creation of paths where there are the best views and the path does not provide continuous views over the adjoining plain, many parts of it being well removed from the scarp, and here the beauty of the route lies in the little secluded valleys which are used instead.

From Filey the route makes for the village of Muston and then swings in a southerly loop across Camp Dale and North Dale and down Ganton Dale by an old earthwork, coming back to the edge of the wolds at Ganton Hall. Now views are opened up northwards across the wide Derwent valley towards the North York Moors until we are within reach of Wintringham and, two miles further on, we reach Settrington. From Settrington the path turns due south over country where the route of the path gives rise to particular difficulty. Established rights of way are infrequent and the creation of new rights of way is not always possible, so that roads and metalled lanes may have to be used. In this area is the site of the medieval village of Wharram Percy and an interesting church as well as fine natural scenery. Thixendale, which follows it, is a narrow waterless valley of exceptional beauty, as is the next dale that we descend to the road at Millington Pasture, a popular picnic spot for motorists. At Kilnwick Percy we overlook the small town of Pocklington, where William Wilberforce was a pupil at the grammar school founded in 1514. We then turn south-east by Warter Priory, with Warter village and its thatched cottages just beyond it. Londnesborough Park now lies below the path. King Edwin of Northumbria had a palace in the village. He was converted to Christianity there, and at nearby Goodmanham there is a stained glass window in the church depicting the event. George Hudson, the nineteenth-century 'railway king', bought the park and had the railway built past his gates, where he had a private station.

The path continues on the wolds above Market Weighton into North Newbald and up Deep Dale, whence it makes its way by further small dales, and along hill-sides with wider views, including views across the Humber, to Welton and thence to North Ferriby. There is a footpath for a large part of the way along the water's edge into the industrial outskirts of Hull.

A Rival to the Pennine Way

The *Cambrian Way* is a proposed high-level route taking in many of the highest of the Welsh mountain peaks, and it would be more challenging and strenuous than the Pennine Way. It could not be achieved except by a person who had had considerable experience on other routes. In these beautiful and lonely hills the chances of accommodation are also few and far between and this is likely to influence the eventual choice of route.

From Cardiff it is proposed that the route should curve round south of the industrial valleys to Pontypool, turning north to the Usk valley at Abergavenny and thence across the Black Mountains on a line close to the Offa's Dyke Path. It would then loop back, recross the Usk valley and traverse the highest summits of the Brecon Beacons westwards to the highest point of the Black Mountains. After descending to Llandovery in the Tywi valley the route would run first up the valley and then across the Elenith and Plynlimon ranges and the wild and lonely area that makes up central Wales, again taking in the highest ground to the Snowdonia National Park. Cader Idris would be approached and climbed from the east, and the path would cross the Barmouth estuary to Maentwrog by way of the Rhinogs peaks, continuing northwards by Moelwyn Mawr and Cnicht and across Nant Gwynant east of Beddgelert on the approach to Snowdonia, descending to the top of the Llanberis pass. The path would then cross Glyder Fawr to Llyn Ogwen, cross the Carnedds, and run straight down to Conway.

A Pennines–Lakeland Link

The *Dales Way* starts at Bradford but could be adapted as a link path

The acorn waymark stands out clearly even amid snow on the Pennine Way (*Crown Copyright*)

between the Pennine Way and the Lake District. It would enable walkers to turn off the Pennine Way at Ribbledale in the Penyghent and Whernside area and to swing north-westwards along the Dent valley instead of northwards to the Roman Wall and Northumberland. The River Dee runs in the Dent valley and the limestone country is attractive where the water foams past great boulders, disappearing occasionally to emerge elsewhere lower down. The route would follow the valley to Dent, a picturesque village with cobbled and winding streets, and Sedburgh, continuing by the Lune valley and westwards across the Howgill Fells to the Lake District at Ambleside. The route might end at this point since once in the Lake District there is no shortage of routes for the walker to follow, but it has been suggested that it might continue northwards along the lower slopes of the Helvellyn range to Keswick and on further to Cockermouth. The Dales Way to the Lake District is already used as a walkers' route but its acceptance as a long distance path would enable improvements to be made since parts of it are at present along public roads where no suitable rights of way are available.

The Cotswolds Way

The *Cotswolds Way* already exists as an escarpment route along the high edge of the Cotswold escarpment with views over the Vale of Evesham and the Severn valley, and it is already signposted. It makes use of roads where pedestrian rights of way are not available in the best places, and therefore does not realise the full potential of the landscape as a scenic route. It ends at Bath in the south and at Chipping Campden in the north, though an extension could be suitably made across lower ground in order to end the route at Stratford on Avon. Attractions of the route, apart from the views, are the old-world villages in mellow stone, ranging across a spectrum of near-white to deep yellow, and the limestone landscape of stone-walled fields.

Other Possible Routes

This by no means exhausts the possible or suggested long distance paths, and the list is a long one. It includes a Thames Riverside Walk; a Saints' Way, from St David's to St Asaph in North Wales; a Welsh Highland Route (both this and the previous suggestion would cover much the same kind of terrain as the Cambrian Way); routes along Roman roads such as the Fosse Way and Sarn Helen; canal routes such as along the Kennet and Avon Canal or the Basingstoke Canal; coast routes in Anglesey and the Isle of Wight; routes along various abandoned railway lines; and many more.

A distinct category of path exists independently in the form of long walkers' routes which are not long distance paths and where the route is therefore in general dictated by the existence of public paths which follow by and large a desired direction, ordinary roads being included where no footpaths can be found to fit into the pattern. The financial support attracted by declaration as a long distance path—for repair, upkeep and improvement and general promotion—is also not payable in these cases though other forms of financial support may be available. Examples of such routes are the Lyke Wake Walk, the Peakway, the Wirral Way and the Tissington Trail, and others are invented from time to time. The Lyke Wake Walk from Osmotherly across the North York Moors to Whitby has become particularly well-known, no doubt because of the strange ritual which attaches to it. As well as having a competitive element, the walk is associated with dirges, coffins, laments, shrouds, night walks and other bizarre features, and badges and certificates in a similar vein can be gained.

It is too soon to say whether these routes will ever officially become long distance paths, the emphasis in the future perhaps being placed on different types of provision, eg routes of a regional or local character as distinct from the national character of the established long distance paths. Such routes, while less rewarding in terms of scenery and achievement, would be less demanding in effort and preparation and would bring the benefits of the open air to larger numbers of people. Routes encircling the conurbations, routes linking local beauty spots or routes along rivers, canals or disused railway lines are examples of this kind. Nevertheless some of the present national paths are clearly incomplete. The South Downs Way is likely to be extended to Winchester, but the Ridgeway Path has no clear western end and could be continued round Salisbury Plain to Shaftesbury, if not as far as the Devon coast. The Cleveland Way does not as yet go as far as Filey. It should also be possible to continue the North Downs Way to meet the South Downs Way at Winchester and the Wolds Way could eventually be continued across the Humber and along the Lincolnshire Wolds to meet the Peddar's Way. A case, if less strong, could be made for continuing some of the coast paths along their respective coastlines. Any idea, however, of linking up the long distance paths and making an integrated, interchange system appears to be misconceived and would do no more than satisfy a sense of tidiness, since it does not take account of landscape realities.

Further development of the existing long distance paths probably lies in a compromise between the need to use a car to see as much as possible in the shortest time with the need actually to get out and walk in order to appreciate the countryside properly. This suggests the making of small unobtrusive parking places near the paths and the designation of return ways by different routes after short or medium-length walks along the long distance path. In order also to introduce more people to the paths who might otherwise think they have nothing of value for them, more on-site information at places of special interest, or information sheets about local history or natural history, would be useful. More general access areas would also have the effect of introducing more of the public to the paths, and map and information boards, direction indicators and seats and shelters might not be inappropriate in certain places. But the proliferation of equipment and advisory notices along the routes is in general to be avoided.

12 · Creating a Long Distance Path

Once the idea for a particular long distance path has been accepted it is necessary to select the route, and for this a survey is required. The general line of the route is determined by the theme adopted for the path, but there is still room for considerable variation. For example, a long inland alternative appears in the Dorset Coast Path to avoid including the whole of Chesil Beach; the historic Offa's Dyke has been abandoned by taking that path across the Black Mountains and the Clwydian Hills; the North Downs Way makes a concession to the Pilgrims' Way by departing from the North Downs and including a spur to Canterbury; and the South Downs bridleway incorporates a footpath alternative to take advantage of the cliff walk between Eastbourne and the Cuckmere. It is sometimes necessary to devise alternatives for times when the main route would be too difficult or to avoid services training areas, and to devise a line which gives reasonable opportunities for refreshments and accommodation and takes in places of interest in the area.

The more immediate object of the survey is, however, by exploration and checking of the selected ground, to devise a route which will best fulfil the basic purpose of providing a scenic route that is not too difficult or too dangerous for the average person to negotiate. In this exercise the point of departure is the maps prepared by the county councils under the 1949 Act showing all the existing rights of way in their area, since existing rights of way will form the basic framework on which the route is constructed. New rights of way will be suggested linking suitable existing rights of way, and this is a task of some responsibility. It would for example be unreasonable to propose a right of way through farm buildings, too close to a private dwelling, diagonally across an arable field, through a young plantation or along the edge of quarry workings.

A variety of agencies have carried out surveys for the Countryside Commission, eg county councils and voluntary organisations such as the Ramblers' Association or the Youth Hostels Association, and individuals have also been commissioned or have volunteered for the purpose. It is then for the Commission to satisfy itself that the route is one for which it can take responsibility having regard not only to its merits in providing access to the countryside but also to such matters as difficulty, safety, and the Countryside Commission's statutory duty to take into account the interests of agriculture and forestry. The Commission is required to consult all the local authorities affected by their proposals, and in practice consults other bodies as well. These may include not only open-air interests such as ramblers, riders and cyclists but public and private bodies concerned with land use, such as the Ministry of Agriculture, the Forestry Commission, the Ministry of Defence, the National Environmental Research Council, the National Farmers' Union and the Timber Growers' Organisation. The comments and criticisms of these bodies should bring to light any inherent conflicts and enable the Commission to form an overall view of the benefits of the proposed route in terms of public enjoyment as against any burdens imposed on landowners and users. It is then for the Commission to attempt to resolve these conflicts and to form its own judgement in pursuit of a line which in the end must be a compromise between the various interests concerned.

There is no provision for public advertisement of proposals for a long distance path, so that individuals affected by a scheme may have no knowledge of the scheme at its formative or approval stages, though information about it could come to their attention through the participation of the local authority at the planning stages or by way of the informal consultations, if any, with their representative organisation. The reason for this is that, so far as existing rights of way are concerned, no additional rights are being taken when a footpath or bridleway is included in a new path (even though increased traffic might be expected), and in the case of a new right of way the matter will be the subject of voluntary negotiation between the landowner and the local authority at a later stage. The landowner can exercise legal rights of objection in the event of a public path order being made. Nevertheless there is an apparent anomaly insofar as the Secretary of State for the Environment approves the scheme, and it is he who later and in the last resort exercises a judicial function in confirming a public path order made by a local authority. The Secretary of State's approval of proposals can therefore be only understood as giving sanction in a general way and not as approval in detail.

Proposals for a long distance path comprise a map showing the proposed line of the path divided into the categories of footpath, bridleway, byeway, road or proposed new path, and a report making recommendations on the construction, maintenance, improvement, signposting and other treatment of the path. The report should also contain a statement of the estimated capital and annual costs of putting the scheme into effect, ie the cost of works and of compensation or other payments to landowners. Information on the cost of work on the paths is obtained from the county councils concerned, who will ultimately be responsible for it. Since the policy is, rightly, to keep the paths as simple and natural as possible, and since land values are, by and large, relatively low in the areas concerned, the capital cost of long distance paths is low, while administrative costs may be relatively high in view of the time-consuming tasks such as negotiating new rights.

Creating New Rights of Way

When proposals are approved by the Secretary of State for the

Stile and signpost used on the paths

Environment it falls to the local authorities to put them into effect. The powers which local authorities operate are in all respects those relating to rights of way in general and there are no powers which relate only to long distance paths as such. If the local authorities do not exercise their powers to implement approved proposals the Secretary of State has powers to require them to do so. The county council, as local highway authority, has responsibility for the construction, upkeep, improvement and safety of all public paths, but both county and district councils have powers for the legal creation of new paths, and it is for them to arrange between them which party is to be responsible for this task. The authority which assumes responsibility must approach the landowner for the dedication of the right of way on his land. Most landowners have readily agreed to dedicate, usually after adjustment of the line to suit their needs, and in these cases a formal agreement is drawn up which may include provision for any stiles and gates needed and for a payment in recognition of the granting of the right of way. Since a dedication is for all time only the freeholder has the ability to dedicate and it is for him to reach accommodation with other persons holding subsidiary interests in the land. It is only rarely after lengthy discussion of all the issues involved that a local authority may, at its discretion, make a public path order, in which case persons with an interest in the land have a right of objection to the Secretary of State for the Environment and may be heard by a person appointed by him before a decision on the order is taken.

These negotiations and procedures necessarily take a long time, particularly as the practice has been to exhaust all possibilities of agreement before a compulsory order is contemplated. Ascertaining proper legal title to land can itself be time-consuming, and local authorities have sometimes been reluctant to press a local owner who has not looked favourably on a request to cede rights over his land. But authorities may create a new path by diverting or closing an existing one, and the farmer may benefit from the realignment. A path cannot be diverted or extinguished by agreement, however, and local or other objections may be made to the order that is made in such cases. Such objections need not be concerned with the long distance path.

The landowner who dedicates a right of way is entitled to a payment which under the compensation code is equivalent to the diminution in the value of the land due to the public right of access arising from the dedication, taking account of any stiles, gates or fences which the local authority has agreed to erect and maintain. The upkeep of these works on existing paths is normally the responsibility of the landowner, for whose purposes they are required. Fencing on a new path is only undertaken exceptionally, where there is a strong agricultural or safety reason, but a farmer may apply the payment he receives to the erection of fencing, if he so wishes. Compensation under a public order is on the same basis as a public path agreement but in this case the landowner is responsible for any stiles, gates or fencing.

It is frequently necessary to vary the line of a long distance path in order to improve it or to take account of land use or other changes. Cliff falls are common on coast routes and when the path disappears the public's right of passage may be extinguished over much longer distances than the cliff fall itself; users' experience may show that the best line was not chosen in the first place; or there may be a favourable opportunity of switching the route to a line which was always desired but is only now available, as when the services give up a training area. A report varying the original proposal may be made to bring the new paths within the same financial and other provisions as the old, and in all respects it follows the same procedures.

Appendix

Useful Addresses

All Paths
The Countryside Commission, John Dower House, Crescent Place,
  Cheltenham, Gloucestershire GL50 3RA
The Ramblers' Association, 1–4 Crawford Mews, London W1H 1PT
The Long Distance Walkers' Association, The Secretary, 11 Thorn Bank,
  Onslow Village, Guildford, Surrey
The Youth Hostels Association, Trevelyan House, 8 St Stephen's Hill,
  St Albans, Hertfordshire

The Pennine Way
The Pennine Way Association, Mr D. Allison, c/o Engineer's and
  Surveyor's Dept., Council Offices, Littleborough, Lancs.

The South West Peninsula Coast Path
The Sou' West Way Association, Assistant Secretary, Kynance, 15 Old
  Newton Road, Kingskerswell, Newton Abbot, Devon

The Offa's Dyke Path
The Offa's Dyke Association, West Street, Knighton, Powys

The Cleveland Way
The Lyke Wake Walk Club, Cleveland Way Secretary, Potto Hill,
  Swainby, Northallerton, Yorkshire

The South Downs Way
The Society of Sussex Downsmen, 93 Church Road, Hove, Sussex

The Ridgeway Path (Chilterns section)
The Chilterns Society, Season's Watch, Bledlow Ridge, High Wycombe,
  Bucks

Bibliography

The Pennine Way

Binns, Alan P. *Walking the Pennine Way* (Gerrard   March 1972)
Marriott, Michael *The Shell Book of the Pennine Way* (Queen Anne Press
   May 1968)
Oldham, Kenneth *The Pennine Way* (Dalesman   March 1974)
Peel, J. H. B. *Along the Pennine Way* (Pan   May 1973)
Stephenson, Tom *The Pennine Way* (HMSO   1970)
Wainwright, A. *The Pennine Way Companion* (Westmorland Gazette
   April 1968)
Wright, C. J. *A Guide to the Pennine Way* (Constable   August 1967)

The Pembrokeshire Coast Path

Barrett, John H. *The Pembrokeshire Coast Path* (HMSO   1974)

The South West Peninsula Coast Path

Marriott, Michael *The Shell Book of the South West Peninsula Path* (Queen
   Anne Press   May 1970)
Pyatt, Edward *Coast Paths of the South West* (David & Charles   June 1971)
Richards, Mark *Walking on the North Cornwall Coastal Footpath* (Thornhill
   October 1974)

Offa's Dyke

Noble, Frank *The Shell Book of the Offa's Dyke Path* (Queen Anne Press
   May 1969)
Wright, C. J. *Offa's Dyke Path* (Constable   1975)

The Cleveland Way

Cowley, Bill *The Cleveland Way* (Dalesman   January 1975)
Falconer, Alan (ed) *The Cleveland Way* (HMSO   March 1972)

The South Downs Way

Teviot, Lord *Walks along the South Downs Way* (Spurbooks   July 1973)

The North Downs Way

Jennett, Sean *The Pilgrims' Way from Winchester to Canterbury* (Cassell   July 1971)

Wright, C. J. *The Pilgrims' Way and North Downs Way* (Constable   June 1971)

The Ridgeway Path

Anderson, J. R. L. *The Oldest Road, an Exploration of the Ridgeway* (Wildwood House   1975)

Other Long Distance Paths

Richards, Mark B. *The Cotswold Way, a Walker's Guide* (Thornhill   March 1973)

Speakman, Colin *The Dales Way* (Dalesman   August 1973)

Index